ERVING GOFFMAN

Decades after his death, the figure of Erving Goffman (1922–82) continues to fascinate. Perhaps the best-known sociologist of the second half of the twentieth century, Goffman was an unquestionably significant thinker whose reputation extended well beyond his parent discipline.

A host of concepts irrevocably linked to Goffman's name – such as 'presentation of self', 'total institutions', 'stigma', 'impression management' and 'passing' – are now staples of a wide range of academic discourses and are slipping into common usage. Goffman's writings uncover a previously unnoticed pattern in the minutiae of everyday interaction. Readers are often shocked when they recognize themselves in his shrewd analyses of errors and common predicaments.

Greg Smith's book traces the emergence of Goffman as a sociological virtuoso, and offers a compact guide both to his sociology and to the criticisms and debates it has stimulated.

Greg Smith teaches at the University of Salford, specializing in ethnographic and interactionist sociology, and sociological and cultural theory. He has published widely on the sociology of Erving Goffman.

KEY SOCIOLOGISTS
Edited by PETER HAMILTON

Now reissued, this classic series provides students with concise and readable introductions to the work, life and influence of the great sociological thinkers. With individual volumes covering individual thinkers, from Emile Durkheim to Pierre Bourdieu, each author takes a distinct line, assessing the impact of these major figures on the discipline as well as the contemporary relevance of their work. These pocket-sized introductions will be ideal for both undergraduates and pre-university students alike, as well as for anyone with an interest in the thinkers who have shaped our time.

Series titles include:

EMILE DURKHEIM
Ken Thompson

THE FRANKFURT SCHOOL AND ITS CRITICS
Tom Bottomore

GEORG SIMMEL
David Frisby

MARX AND MARXISM
Peter Worsley

MAX WEBER
Frank Parkin

MICHEL FOUCAULT
Barry Smart

PIERRE BOURDIEU
Richard Jenkins

SIGMUND FREUD
Robert Bocock

ZYGMUNT BAUMAN
Tony Blackshaw

AUGUSTE COMTE
Mike Gane

ERVING GOFFMAN
Greg Smith

ERVING GOFFMAN

GREG SMITH

LONDON AND NEW YORK

First Indian Reprint, 2015

First published 2006
by Routledge
2 Park Square, Milton Park, Abingdon, Oxon OX14 4RN

Simultaneously published in the USA and Canada
by Routledge
711 Third Ave, New York, NY 10017

*Routledge is an imprint of the Taylor & Francis Group, an informa
business*

© 2006 Greg Smith

Typeset in Times New Roman by
HWA Text and Data Management Ltd, Tunbridge Wells
Printed and bound in India by Bhavish Graphics.

British Library Cataloguing in Publication Data
A catalogue record for this book is available from the British
Library

Library of Congress Cataloging in Publication Data
A catalog record for this book has been requested

ISBN10: 0–415–35591–5 (pbk)
ISBN10: 0–203–00723–9 (ebk)

ISBN13: 978–0–415–35591–9 (pbk)
ISBN13: 978–0–203–00723–5 (ebk)

For sale in India, Pakistan, Nepal, Bhutan, Bangladesh and Sri Lanka only.

Table of Contents

Acknowledgements

My thinking about the ideas discussed in this book has benefited from discussions with Elaine Baldwin, Mike Ball, Gary Alan Fine, Carol Brooks Gardner, Bill Gronfein, David Jary, Brian Longhurst, Phil Manning, Rob Philburn, Tom Scheff, Wes Sharrock, Andrew Travers, Fran Waksler, Rod Watson, Doug Webster, Robin Williams and Yves Winkin. A version of Chapter 7 was presented at the Couch-Stone Symposium of the Society for the Study of Symbolic Interaction, University of Las Vegas, in February 1999. Kathy Charmaz made particularly helpful comments on that occasion. My thanks also to Mary Byrne, who assisted with the preparation of the manuscript. Once again, I am grateful to Shauna Smith for bearing the vagaries of my academic ways with more tolerance than I had any right to expect.

1

Goffman's Project

A SOCIOLOGICAL ENIGMA

Erving Goffman was one of the twentieth century's most remarkable practitioners of social science, a sociologist universally acknowledged for his singular talent. Long after his death in 1982, simple mention of the word 'Goffman' is enough to signify not just a subject matter but also a highly distinctive attitude and analytic stance toward the social world. He first came to prominence with the 1959 publication of *The Presentation of Self in Everyday Life*, which he followed two years later with the even more influential *Asylums*. Unusually, for a sociologist, Goffman enjoyed fame outside his home discipline. That fame was curious because Goffman was not interested, as many leading sociologists are, in the big questions about the nature and development of modern society. His interest was in the structure of face-to-face interaction, in the minutiae of ordinary talk and activity. His sociology was not theoretically ambitious. It modestly espoused description, classification and conceptual articulation, and showed no aspiration towards propositional expression as fully-fledged explanatory and predictive theory. Nor did Goffman develop a school of thought or a new methodological approach for the study of social life. Rather, his interests were confined to quite narrow concerns with what he called the 'interaction order' and its implications for the self. Goffman's single-minded pursuit of the analysis of interaction and what that analysis suggested about the selves of participants in interaction ('interactants'), published in 11 books and numerous articles from the mid-1950s to the early 1980s, won him many admirers (and not a few critics) across academic sociology and beyond.

The writings of Erving Goffman have always attracted extremes of assessment. While many readers have been intrigued and delighted by the acuity of his observations and by his matchless analyses of ordinary social life, others have despaired over Goffman's work, finding it a specious evasion of the serious theoretical, technical and moral issues that have animated sociology since its inception. Overlaying these responses is a widespread puzzlement about the broad character of Goffman's project, which in substance, approach and detail did not obviously resemble any of the major forms of sociological work practised in the middle of the twentieth century.

Notwithstanding the popularity and attractiveness of Goffman's sociological writings, there are many readers and commentators who express degrees of bafflement about his overall enterprise. For these readers his sociology constitutes an 'enigma' (a recurrent term in the critical literature). They understand what they have read adequately enough – after all his work enjoys wide popular appeal because it is accessible and capable of engaging the non-specialist. But readers often have difficulty in grasping the immediate or larger point of it all or in locating the work within the wider perspectives and debates of sociology and the human sciences.

Goffman's rapid rise in the early 1960s coincided with a period of great change in American sociology. The certainties provided by structural-functionalism and empirical theory were increasingly challenged by the renaissance of Marxist sociology and the rise of novel interpretive sociological perspectives such as phenomenology, symbolic interactionism, and ethnomethodology. The interpretive perspectives were often buttressed by new thinking in ordinary language philosophy and the philosophy of science. Goffman's sociology played an important part in these changes, more as an exemplar of alternative conceptions of sociological practice than itself a source of theoretical critique. Not only did Goffman seem to offer a good case in point of a non-positivistic sociology, it was seen also as a symptom of the actual or impending crisis of the discipline in the 1960s (Gouldner 1970). Of course, Goffman's success owed at least as much to his shrewd observational talent and his wit and grace as a writer as it did the concrete findings the texts delivered. His writing successfully married the novelist's eye for the detail and particularity of human conduct with the systematizing drive of the social scientist. Here it seemed was a sociologist with the literary sensibility and observational skills to uncover the ironies and discrepancies to which interactional conduct seemed susceptible, wherever it occurred.

The distinctive cast of Goffman's thinking about social life was evident in his subtle and skilful use of a range of metaphors (dramaturgical, ritual, game theoretical, ethological) and his flair for sardonic witticism and ironic observation. It was also expressed in the highly individual look of many of the pages of his books. Goffman was not afraid to illustrate his ideas with quotations from novels, first person accounts and newspaper reports. Yet he was no mere popularizer. Goffman was immensely well read; many pages of his books are heavy with substantial footnotes that reference specialized academic sources to support or qualify his analyses. The manner in which Goffman undertook the project of the sociology of the interaction order was every bit as striking as its substance. Goffman's sociological style, as well as the substantive claims his sociology advanced, helped to make him an enduringly controversial figure.

Goffman's sociology provoked numerous interpretations, testimony to the ambiguous legacy his work represents. The critical literature suggests a host of dichotomies informing his writings. Are they best seen as structuralist or symbolic interactionist, formalist or phenomenological, modernist or postmodernist, Machiavellian or existentialist, realist or empiricist? While Goffman's ideas cannot be reduced to any one of these categories, they nonetheless capture some of the tensions and ambiguities of his sociological thinking. Acquaintances of Goffman tell of how he enjoyed testing the limits of the rules and understandings shaping face-to-face conduct in restaurants, cinema queues, lecture theatres and living rooms. Yet such sociologically-inspired mischievousness was matched by a contrary impulse, an almost Durkheimian regard for the power of ritual and routine to shape our thought, feelings and conduct. Goffman was, as Bennett Berger (1986: xvii) once put it, part 'Nietzschean moral adventurer', part 'prudent Victorian'.

Some of these tensions and ambiguities were reflected in Goffman's own reputation and career. He was the maverick outsider who eventually became President of the American Sociological Association. Add to this the mystery Goffman created around his persona by refusing many of the trappings of the celebrity intellectual. He very reluctantly and infrequently consented to interview. He never appeared on radio or television, and he discouraged attempts to record his voice or photograph his image. Dell Hymes (1984), a longstanding colleague of Goffman's, wrote of 'Erving's gift', of the unique sociological talent he possessed and the difficulties that Goffman had in coming to terms with it. As the corpus of Goffman's writings grew in the 1960s and 1970s, it became increasingly apparent that an unusual contribution to understanding the human condition was in progress.

INTERPRETIVE PROBLEMS IN READING GOFFMAN

Goffman's major achievement was to demonstrate how the particulars of the conduct of 'co-present' persons, that is persons who are physically present to one another, are amenable to sociological analysis. He saw his work as a preliminary foray into a sociologically uncharted territory that might lead to further, more systematic and precise investigations of interaction. For Goffman, the first and perhaps only proper concern for the professional sociologist (or 'student of society', his favoured phrase) was the investigation of society (see Verhoeven 1993). With such an ambition, it has to be said that a book like this – a study of a sociologist rather than social reality – would probably have appalled Goffman. For Goffman the study of the ideas of sociologists made an empirical discipline into a literary one and, worse, was likely to promote the uncritical canonization of the eminent rather than the critical application and development of their ideas. To construe an individual sociologist's life and writings as an object of academic attention was, Goffman once claimed (David 1980), 'a low form of hero worship'. This explains in part why Goffman was a reluctant interviewee (there are only three interviews of substance in the public domain: David 1980; Winkin 1984; Verhoeven 1993). He hoped that his publications would speak and be judged for themselves, since they contained the clearest statements of his ideas, which subsequent conversation would be unlikely to illuminate further. (Nevertheless, statements made by Goffman about Goffman usefully illuminate the nature of his exceptional sociological project.) Goffman's diffidence about open engagement in print with his critics can be understood in similar terms. The real work for sociologists, he felt, lay elsewhere, in the investigation of the features of the social world. As he testily observed in the paper that was his sole direct reply to critics, 'pronouncing and counter-pronouncing are not the study of society' (1981b: 61). He once told Stanford Lyman (personal communication 1992) 'sociology is something that you do, not something that you read'.

Various constructions might be placed upon these remarks. The sceptical might regard them as a thinly-veiled attempt to enhance the status of an already enigmatic sociology, a deflecting tactic designed to discourage close reflection upon the nature and adequacy of a contentious sociological project. Confronted with the puzzle of how to make sense of Goffman, the puzzle's originator tells us our troubles are not worth pursuing (or at least, not worth pursuing into print). Goffman may well be right to caution sociologists about the very real risk of goal-displacement inherent in critical reflection upon any piece of sociological work, but the admonition should not be taken too literally. For if Goffman's work is to be understood and applied by others in anything more than a piecemeal fashion, if it is to be fully capitalized upon and developed, then critical appreciation is an important preliminary – an endeavour not necessarily at odds with the empirical investigations that Goffman wants to encourage.

Other features of Goffman's writings serve to make critical commentary an exacting task. He was less willing than most of his readers to regard his intellectual product as a 'unitary thing' and explicitly called into question the neat, uniform characterization of his writings as 'Goffman's sociology'. Goffman agreed that there must be some continuity running through his writings, since one author can produce only so many ideas, but he also suggested that speaking of his sociology in the singular is a convenient gloss that disguises real inconsistencies across his writings (David 1980).

It is certainly true that others spoke more readily and more confidently of 'Goffman's sociology' than did its author. Very early on in Goffman's career it became evident that his writings displayed a distinctive sociological attitude and that there was enough consistency in his analytical procedures to warrant the use of the 'Goffman's sociology' and the adjectives 'Goffmanian' and 'Goffmanesque' (the latter first used in print in 1956). Yet for an author whose work was informed by a clear vision of social life and guided by a sure sense of its potential, his *oeuvre* lacks self-evident internal coherence. Each of his books is written, as Wes Sharrock (1976) noted, as if none of the others had been. Each starts from conceptual scratch and, even where there are apparently substantial overlaps, contains little cross-referencing to ideas contained in earlier work (a deficiency that Goffman did begin to remedy in his later writings). Indexes are absent or less than adequate. Goffman's facility for inventing new terms and rendering those of other writers grist to his analytical mill seems to efface his own earlier usages, subverting any bid to form a system built around a conceptual core. And to make matters more difficult, Goffman provides the most minimal guidance to readers about how his work might be situated in relation to established sociological traditions and issues. Understandably enough, this has been seen as a curious way in which to develop a new area of sociology, particularly one that was pre-eminently concerned with conceptual articulation.

THE ORDERLINESS OF FACE-TO-FACE INTERACTION

The development of a new field of sociology remained Goffman's paramount project, famously stating that 'my ultimate interest is to develop the study of face-to-face interaction as a naturally bounded, analytically coherent field – a sub-area of sociology' (1969a: ix). In what he knew would be his last word on the matter, 'The interaction order' (1983a) (the posthumously published Presidential Address to the American Sociological Association), Goffman noted that face-to-face interaction is a domain of social life characterized by 'co-presence'. Whenever we are present before others – or are in their 'response presence' – we convey to them something of ourselves through the content of our talk ('expressions given') and through the manner of our talk, through our posture, glances, our apparent disposition, and so forth ('expressions given off' or 'exuded'). As Goffman (1981a: 2) points out, every sane adult is 'wonderfully accomplished' at producing these expressions and at appreciating their significance. In the presence of others there is no time out, no escape from the implications of the person's expressivity: even complete silence and immobility conveys something to others about the person. Thus the substantive focus of Goffman's sociology is the 'comingling' that occurs in 'social situations', defined specifically as those environments where 'two or more persons are in one another's response presence' (1983a: 2).

Goffman considers the field of face-to-face interaction to be 'naturally bounded' (1969a: ix) by characteristics that seem to apply in all places and at all times. Interaction has a 'promissory, evidential character' that facilitates our ordinary capacity to make inferences from the expressions given and given off by others. But there are other, no less important general features. Face-to-face activities – an after-dinner speech, a courtesy extended to another – are circumscribed in time and space, hence one of Goffman's favoured terms for them: 'small behaviors'. Much interactional activity has little or no latent phase, so that to postpone an activity (e.g. responding to a question) can be highly consequential for the subsequent course of the interaction. There is a distinct 'psychobiological' dimension to face-to-face interaction: the biological and psychological make up of the person is centrally implicated, so that at the very least the attention of interactants is required, and often also an appropriate emotional stance, bodily orientation and perhaps even physical effort. It follows, says Goffman that personal territory (in both the physical and psychological sense) is of considerable importance.

The natural boundedness of interaction is ultimately provided by the expressive, communicative, perceptual and physical capacities of the human species. These embodied properties set very obvious limits to what can transpire interactionally: we can only see a facial expression or hear a speaker's talk when within a perceptual range established by our species' sensory capacities; as adults we are unlikely to take seriously the violent threats of a three-year-old, and so forth. Within these very broad confines a diverse range of interactional conduct is possible. More generally Goffman suggests that the physical capacities of human agents both enable and constrain the forms that interaction can take, a notion he was later to take up under the heading of 'system requirements' (1981a: 14–15).

What is so special about face-to-face situations? Consider what may take place there:

> … it is in social situations that individuals can communicate in the fullest sense of the term, and it is only in them that individuals can coerce one another, assault one another, importune one another gesturally, give physical comfort, and so forth. Moreover, it is in social situations that most of the world's work gets done. (1979: 5–6).

For Goffman the interaction order was an identifiable, naturally bounded domain of social life, worthy of study simply 'because it is there' (1983a: 17). Little further rationale for its study is expressly claimed. 'Most of the world's work' occurs in social situations, and Goffman (1963a: 248) further ventures that there is also an important sense in which people 'belong' to encounters more than to any family, class, gender or nation. Goffman's reluctance to make any *theoretical* capital out of these observations is notable. He carefully avoided any suggestion that face-to-face situations are paramount in human experience (a central motif of *Frame Analysis*) or that they provide the micro foundations on which macroscopic sociological phenomena rest (e.g. Goffman 1983a: 8-9). His argument was simply that the interaction order exists, alongside the political order, the economic order and so forth, and the present point in history affords us the intellectual and practical resources to study it sociologically. The unwillingness to make any grand theoretical claims for the primacy of the interaction order undoubtedly disappointed some commentators (e.g. Burns 1992: 28-32) but this disinclination connects with Goffman's contention that the interaction order enjoys a relative autonomy vis-à-vis other social orders.

Goffman also seeks to lend 'analytical coherence' to the study of interaction using principles and ideas drawn from the discipline of sociology. Interaction is much more a matter of *social* competence than we often believe. One of Goffman's major accomplishments was to demonstrate that interaction has a social organization amenable to sociological investigation. His most fundamental analytic conception is that interaction can be treated as a species of social order. Just as a society can be regarded as organized by a political order, a kinship order, an economic order and so on, so too it could be shown to exhibit an interaction order. The dismissive labelling of his work as mere social psychology is misleading since it underplays the strongly sociological undercurrent of his reasoning. While the 'social psychology' label usefully picks up on Goffman's long interest in the self, the overall thrust of his work is to treat interaction as a reality in its own right in which issues concerning self are approached from the point of view of the workings of interactions, relationships and organizations. In this regard Goffman offers a sociological respecification of G.H. Mead's empirically-oriented but essentially philosophical doctrine of 'social behaviorism'. Self and interaction, Goffman's work repeatedly shows, are not topics that sociology needs to cede to another discipline. One example of the clearly sociological direction of Goffman's reasoning can be found in an early paper where he employs the fashionable functionalist language of the time to describe interaction as 'a little social system with its own boundary-maintaining tendencies' (1967: 113). Interaction is treated as socially organized or socially ordered: its constituent elements, processes and acts (the content and tone of the talk, the physical appearance of interactants, their posture, glances, etc.) are understood to be arranged and related in socially defined, socially sanctioned ways. In analysing interaction in itself – not in terms of its determinants, not in terms of its outcomes – Goffman is able to show how the various constituent elements of interaction are socially arranged and collectively coordinated in the production of encounters. These orienting conceptions fuel the sociology distinctively linked to Goffman's name.

BIOGRAPHICAL SKETCH

Erving Manual Goffman was born on 11 June 1922 in the village of Mannville, Alberta, the son of Jewish immigrants from the Ukraine (Winkin 1988 provides a comprehensive account of Goffman's life through to 1959). Over 200,000 Ukrainians migrated to Canada in the two decades leading up to the outbreak of World War I. When Erving and his older sister Frances were small their parents moved the family some 500 miles east, first to Dauphin, Manitoba, then to Winnipeg. Goffman's father ran a clothing store and the business was prosperous enough to underwrite Goffman's education through to the end of graduate school. Goffman went to high school in Winnipeg and in September 1939 entered the University of Manitoba (also in Winnipeg) to major in chemistry. During the three years Goffman spent at the University of Manitoba, his academic interests gradually shifted towards the social sciences.

After Manitoba Goffman moved to Toronto, where he worked at the Canadian National Film Board. Dennis Wrong encouraged him to return to university to complete a BA degree at the University of Toronto in 1945. In the autumn of that year he moved south to enrol as a graduate student at the University of Chicago. The transition to graduate work was not straightforward. It was four years before he obtained the MA degree. In 1949 he was able to continue his Chicago studies towards a PhD, courtesy of the Social Anthropology Department at the University of Edinburgh, who supported the fieldwork he undertook in Shetland between 1949–51.

Goffman married Angelica Choate in 1952 and spent part of that year in Paris, writing up his Shetland findings. Their son was born the following year. Following the award of his doctorate in December 1953, Goffman was able to spend another year at the University of Chicago, working with William Soskin of the Psychology Department on a study of the characteristics of social interaction. Late in 1954 Goffman became a Visiting Scientist at the National Institute of Mental Health, Bethesda, Maryland. In this post Goffman undertook fieldwork at St. Elizabeths Hospital, Washington D.C., made famous by *Asylums* (1961a). At the beginning of 1958, Goffman was appointed Assistant Professor in the Department of Sociology at the University of California, Berkeley, then chaired by Herbert Blumer. The publication of five books over the next five years ensured his rapid promotion to full Professor. These included *The Presentation of Self in Everyday Life*, which won him the 1961 MacIver Award for the best book in American sociology, as well as *Asylums* (1961a) and *Stigma* (1963b), the books that gave Goffman a public profile, allying him to the new labelling theories of deviance and the anti-psychiatry movement.

While at Berkeley, Goffman began fieldwork in the casinos of Nevada, initially as a customer and later working as a dealer. At Berkeley he influenced a number of graduate students, including John Lofland, Gary Marx, Harvey Sacks, Dorothy Smith and David Sudnow. His wife Angelica, who had serious mental problems, took her own life in 1964. Goffman spent 1966–1967 as a Visiting Fellow at Harvard University, which facilitated dialogue with game theorist, Thomas Schelling (an economics Nobel prize-winner in 2005). In 1968 he took up a position as Benjamin Franklin Professor of Anthropology and Sociology at the University of Pennsylvania. Colleagues there included Dell Hymes and William Labov, both of whom stimulated the sociolinguistic dimensions of his work seen most clearly in his last book, *Forms of Talk*. A cohort of feminist-oriented students at Pennsylvania, including Carol Gardner, stimulated Goffman's interests in gender issues (*Gender Advertisements*,

1979). In 1981 he married linguistics professor Gillian Sankoff, with whom he had a daughter in 1982. His death from stomach cancer in November 1982 came at the end of a year in which he had served as President of the American Sociological Association.

OUTLINE OF THE BOOK

Where did Goffman's unique sociological worldview come from? While Goffman certainly was an original, it is important to remember that his sociology did not materialize out of nowhere. Chapter 2 traces the first stages of the development of Goffman's ideas through his earliest writings to his doctoral dissertation, 'Communication Conduct in an Island Community' (1953). It explores some of the early and abiding influences on his sociological thinking in the postwar University of Chicago milieu, showing how they impact on his earliest published work. In sketching Goffman the embryonic sociologist, some key and lasting influences and traditions shaping his ideas come into relief. By the time he obtained his doctorate in 1953, 'Goffman' had emerged with his first full-blown account of the sociology of the interaction order.

The following four chapters examine the substance of his sociology beginning with an outline of the basic elements or 'units' of the interaction order that are mainly contained writings published in the decade or so after Goffman's dissertation. The next chapter considers how the notion of 'frame' revitalized Goffman's later sociology, deepening his perspective to accommodate more fully experiential concerns about our sense of reality. Ordinary experience can be framed in a number of ways – as literal, figurative, playful, fabricated and so on. The chapter explores the development of this idea in *Frame Analysis* (1974) and considers its refinement as a key element of his late analysis of talk's forms, concentrating on the notion of footing.

Of course, Goffman was not only concerned with developing a general sociology of interaction and experience. The next two chapters consider what might be seen as the 'applied', 'social problems-oriented' Goffman. The compelling treatments of mental patients in *Asylums* (1961a) and the socially excluded in *Stigma* (1963b) introduced his ideas to audiences who did not routinely read sociology. Later, in the 1970s, Goffman would offer his own distinctive take on the gender issues brought to the fore by feminists. Like Durkheim and Freud, Goffman believed that much could be learned about normal social conduct by carefully considering its abnormal forms. Throughout his career Goffman wrote about persons whose identities in social situations were different, other than expected, and often problematic (mental patients and the mentally ill, the stigmatized, women in the Simone de Beauvoir, 'woman as other' sense). In these studies of the interactional dynamics of difference, otherness and exclusion (Goffman had severe reservations about common sociological uses of 'deviance'), Goffman's moral preoccupations come to the fore. These two chapters examine the sociological bases of that distinctive moral sensibility.

The questions these studies raise about self and identity are taken further in the following chapter. While the interaction order formed the ostensible focus of Goffman's sociology, in all his writings the notion of the self is an unavoidable referent. Goffman showed how self was crucially shaped by the moment-to-moment flow of events at the interactional level. This chapter reviews the formulations of the individual that Goffman presents and considers some of the issues they raise. For Goffman self cannot be eliminated from the proper study of interaction. Goffman is seen to produce a sociological account of the person that is sensitive both to rational, calculative elements and to human emotions.

The chapter on method and textuality raises questions about doing sociology Goffman's way. Many would question whether Goffman had a method in any of its usual senses. Unlike almost every other major twentieth-century sociologist, Goffman cared little about expansive disquisition on method, fearing that actual practice would always be at variance with stated principles (Becker 2003). Yet his work displays a subtle awareness of key methodological questions. Goffman's broad approach to sociological inquiry, emphasizing qualitative and interactionist precepts and taking a classificatory approach that reworks Simmel's formal method, is discussed. However, the power of Goffman's sociology did not simply rest on his approach and methods. Goffman was a stylish writer in a discipline noted for its literary gracelessness. In Goffman the analytical and the textual, the sociologist and the writer, substance and style, are closely intertwined. Goffman's peerless command of the sociological uses of metaphor and irony are essential constituents of the analyses he develops and the persuasiveness of his texts. Finally, the conclusion briefly surveys the influence of Goffman's sociology and gives an estimate of his continuing relevance to a range of sociologically-oriented enquiries.

Overall, this book seeks to provide an account of the leading themes and logic of Goffman's approach. It locates these ideas in some of the debates making up his undeniable though often ambiguous legacy to sociology and neighbouring disciplines.

2
Origins and Emergence

Imagine this. It is a windy, early spring evening in 1950 in Baltasound, a village on Unst, the most northerly of the Shetland Isles. A small, stockily-built 27-year-old Canadian student has walked a couple of hundred metres across a wet field from the only hotel on the island, where he hass been helping out in the kitchen, to the small, single-storey cottage he has just bought from Wally Priest, a local crofter. Wally's fiancée, Mary, also works at the hotel. Mary, Wally and many other villagers get on well with the student who arrived on the boat from Lerwick the previous December, when the first winter snow was in the air. However, they are puzzled about what he is doing here. He stays longer than the visitors who come to birdwatch or fish or who are simply intrigued by the village's remote location. Some think he is studying the economics of croft agriculture. Others have heard him say that he is an anthropologist. A few villagers call him Erving to his face and Goffman (not Mr Goffman as would be proper) behind his back. He is willing to make himself useful, casting peats with Wally to provide winter fuel as well as lending a hand in the hotel kitchen. When he first arrived he lived in the hotel, but now he just takes his meals there. He is approachable and open. At the hotel, the cook and the scullery boy (a young lad just out of school) sometimes take their breaks with Erving in his cottage. He does not seem to have any 'side' to him. He does not take advantage or complain, even when he has cause to (about, for instance, the hotel food – the cook's skills are very variable and there are far too many dishes that come caked in bright orange breadcrumbs). First thing most mornings he walks the half mile or so down to the village post office to collect his mail. There and in the village store he is always ready to chat with anyone. He walks a lot, always in those knee-high leather boots he must have brought with him from Canada, sometimes taking photographs with a nice-looking German camera. No-one is quite sure how he spends his afternoons. Reading probably – the cottage is stuffed with large numbers of books he has had shipped over. But he is no recluse. He is a regular at the evening socials held fortnightly from September to March at the village hall. He can certainly hold his drink when men in their twos and threes nip out of the hall (which is not licensed) for a swig of home-made hooch.

That evening Erving Goffman gets back to the cottage after helping wash the hotel's dinner pots and dishes. He types a few notes about the evening's kitchen gossip. Then he settles down to read a couple of chapters of the new murder mystery his sister sent him last week. Tomorrow he will give some more thought to just what exactly he will put into the PhD dissertation that he has come to Baltasound to research. His mentor, W. Lloyd Warner, is expecting a case study of the island community, along the lines of his very successful series of books about 'Yankee City'. But Erving Goffman does not want to do just another ethnography – the Chicago sociology department has turned out enough of those these past 30 years. He has a sneaking admiration for Talcott Parsons' work, even though it is not popular with many Chicago sociology professors. He is intrigued by the possibility of doing something novel, something that employs his special aptitude for noticing the details of people's interpersonal conduct. His Chicago classmates nickname him 'the little dagger' because of his talent for the pointed personal comment. Sometimes, they felt, he never knew when to stop.

The world Goffman encounters on Unst is very different from the city of Chicago. Its remoteness and open spaces may have reminded him of rural Canada. In 1950 the island was home to a little over a thousand people and a rather larger number of sheep. Roughly 9 miles long and 4 miles wide, it is famous for having provided novelist Robert Louis Stevenson with the outline for his map of Treasure Island. You are never far from the sea. The rolling landscape is open, treeless and windswept. Its latitude is further north than Stockholm and St Petersburg, so days are very short around mid-winter. While there is still rationing for basic foodstuffs in the UK, here there is always plenty of fish and mutton and the sailors who pass through regularly have goods to trade or sell (Winkin 2000; Priest 1998).

No-one can say for sure, but it seems likely that Goffman first worked out the idea of the sociology of the interaction order when he was living in that cottage in Baltasound. If he came with the idea of doing a Warneresque community study, by the time he left in May 1951 he seems to have developed other ideas. This isolated community was well suited to Goffman's new purpose. It offered a wide range of interaction combined with the ready availability of background information about the participants (Goffman 1953a: 7). Baltasound became Goffman's 'natural laboratory' for the study of interaction practices. Robert E. Park and Ernest W. Burgess, founders of the original Chicago School of sociology had devised the notion of the city as a natural laboratory in the 1920s. They recommended an observational, anthropological approach to the practices and conceptions of life displayed by the groups, communities and cultures of the contemporary city. Goffman creatively developed this established Chicagoan methodological theme. Baltasound stood to Goffman's new sociological project as the city of Chicago had done to an earlier generation of urban ethnographers. In light of the later criticism that Goffman's sociology reflected attitudes and behaviours characteristic of the modern, urban, corporate world, it is ironic that its basic conceptions were founded on an investigation of village life.

What led this Canadian student, studying for a doctorate at one of the USA's most prestigious sociology departments, to undertake fieldwork in a location as remote as can be found in the UK? To understand the configuration of interests and associations that led Goffman to this remote island, we need to sketch his early education. By tracing the influences Goffman encountered and the interests he pursued as a graduate student we can better situate claims about Goffman's sociological genius. Goffman was unquestionably a singular figure in the history of sociology but that singularity was not produced overnight. Its origins lie in Goffman's imaginative synthesis of ideas encountered during his third decade. As a 20-year-old in 1942, Goffman left the University of Manitoba without completing his science degree but having acquired an unanticipated interest in social science. Ten years later, the 30-year-old embroiled in the completion of his doctoral dissertation was beginning a sociological project that would leave an indelible mark on the history of sociology.

GOFFMAN BEFORE CHICAGO

After Manitoba, Goffman was employed by the Canadian National Film Board in Ottawa. Goffman's contribution to the war effort was to work for an agency then heavily involved in the production of propaganda films. At that time the noted Scottish documentary filmmaker, John Grierson

(1898–1972) directed the Board. While Goffman's duties were mainly low-level and routine (boxing films for despatch and preparing cuttings files from magazines), he could not have avoided exposure to discussions about filmic practices for decomposing ordinary life into elements that could then be reconstructed as a representation of reality (Winkin 1988: 20–1). While at the National Film Board, Goffman met Dennis Wrong, a recent sociology graduate of the University of Toronto, who urged him to restart his studies (Wrong 1990: 9). Bringing forward his Manitoba credits, Goffman enrolled at the University of Toronto in early 1944 and graduated in November 1945.

At Toronto Goffman took courses in sociology. Perhaps his two most influential teachers were C.W.M. Hart and Ray Birdwhistell. Hart, an Australian, had thoroughly absorbed the Durkheimian perspective from Radcliffe-Brown at the University of Sydney in the late 1920s and applied it to his fieldwork material among the Tiwi of northern Australia. From Hart, Goffman obtained initial exposure to Durkheim, who was to be a major and lasting influence on his thought. Goffman also took classes with the young Ray Birdwhistell (1918–1994). At Toronto he had already begun his immensely detailed investigations of the symbolic significance of human body-motion and gesture (see Birdwhistell 1971) that he would name 'kinesics'. Speaking in 1980, Goffman recalled how much Birdwhistell's innovatory project had impressed him (Winkin 1984). In the early 1950s, when Goffman began developing the sociology of the interaction order in earnest, Birdwhistell's kinesics would represent an exemplar of attention to the minute detail of human conduct. In 1945 that interaction sociology was still a long way off. Some of its eventual contours doubtless originate in Goffman's undergraduate education in wartime Canada. According to Elizabeth Bott Spillius (personal communication), even as an undergraduate Goffman was 'formidably observant' and a voracious reader who just needed some stimuli and guidance to shape his idiosyncratic way of viewing the world. Graduate school in postwar Chicago was to provide the context for that development.

Goffman's early work can be organized under three headings: first, a rejection of conventional experimental method, the product of his reflections upon his MA thesis research; second, early publications that establish an interest in discrepancies between appearances and realities and firm up his developing ethnographically gilded formal sociology; third, the PhD dissertation, which represents his first effort to systematically assay the interaction order.

THE MASTERS THESIS: ABANDONING METHOD?

In the research components of both his masters and PhD degrees Goffman does the unexpected. His master's thesis of 1949 shows him grappling with issues arising from the application of a traditional positivistic research design grounded in the logic of experimental method. Toward the end of his first year as a graduate student at Chicago, Goffman devised a thesis proposal to examine the relationship between social class and personality. The research was directed by W. Lloyd Warner, an anthropologist turned analyst of the American class structure (see Warner 1988) and William E. Henry, an expert in cultural applications of the then relatively new psychological instrument, the Thematic Apperception Test (TAT).

Goffman originally conceived his research as an adjunct to Warner and Henry's investigation of the audience for 'Big Sister', a popular daytime radio serial (Warner and Henry, 1948). In 1945 they began collecting data from wives of skilled and white-collar workers. As a beginning graduate student, Goffman was caught up in his advisors' enthusiasm to explore the potential of the new test. Consequently, Goffman devised a research plan that would focus instead on a sample of wives of professional and managerial workers. In autumn 1946, he interviewed 50 women from the Hyde Park district of Chicago with the TAT.

Goffman's plan to explore the relationship between class and personality with this sample of 'HP subjects' did not work out in its original form. The thesis is a densely written piece that explains why the original objectives could not be attained and offers an alternative analysis of the research interviews. Goffman's first substantial work gives clues about why he came to adopt an exploratory, essayistic and classificatory sociological approach. Goffman discovered a number of problems in executing the original research design in accordance with the principles of scientific research. The chief problem was how to assure reliable interpretation of TAT responses (Smith 2003). The TAT is a projective test that works by exposing subjects to a series of deliberately ambiguous pictures. The subject is invited to construct a story around each picture. The inventors of this test believed these stories – the 'responses to depicted experience' of the thesis's title – were projections of the subject's inner person, an X-ray of the inner self. Goffman argued that there was no methodical, consistent way of making these deductions from subjects' actual test responses. Goffman concluded that the TAT was inadequate as a systematic instrument to measure the personality variable. Then Goffman discovered that his collection of interviews was less a sample and more a loose-knit social network. The original plan to examine the class-personality relationship fell through.

Goffman proceeds to salvage an analysis by approaching the TAT interview as an example of what he would later call an encounter. He distinguishes 'direct' responses, where the subject responds to the picture on the test card as if it was a real event, from 'indirect' responses, which include 'all statements which manage by some means or other to avoid the obligation of assuming the momentary "reality" of the representations' (Goffman 1949: 47). A direct response can be avoided in three ways: 'sympathy', 'content' and 'representation'. HP subjects would sometimes refuse to communicate the sympathy conventionally demanded by a picture; or their response would refuse to engage the manifest content of the picture; or the pictures themselves would be interpreted as aesthetic objects. These methods of refusing to fully engage the test situation anticipate conduct he would later make famous as 'role distance'. The pervasiveness of indirect responses troubled Goffman. He concludes that the appetite for vicarious experience of HP subjects is 'jaded'.

While interviewing Hyde Park wives in their own homes Goffman also surreptiously gathered data on living room furnishings. He identifies a 'pattern of disengagement', congruent with the indirect response, evident in the disruption of conventional 'sacred' definitions of the living room: by the combination of eighteenth-century and modern furniture, by the use of bright wall paint, and by the visible presence of utility items such as typewriters and filing cabinets. Already, in 1949, recognizably 'Goffmanesque' locutions and ironies can be found:

> In many living rooms the ritual of order and cleanliness was nicely
> violated by the permitted presence of a dog, a child, a huge toy, or a
> fireplace-basket of coal or wood … subjects frequently admitted that
> they knew nothing about furniture, and in some cases this seemed
> to be an honest statement of fact. (1949: 69)

Departures from conventional definitions of living room furnishings parallel the departures from the standard conventions of interpersonal conduct:

> subjects seemed to make a point of carefully violating, once or twice,
> the traditional proprieties of conversation; this involved conspicuous
> use of colloquialisms, direct references to sex, and polite use of
> impolite profanities … sometimes HP subjects disposed their body
> and limbs in a way that did not convey the maximum of restraint; this
> involved wide gestures of hand and arm, standing poses of several
> kinds, and conspicuously comfortable sitting positions. These
> movements seemed to be a sign that the subject was in control of

her inhibitions, rather than a sign that impulses were in control of the subject. (1949: 70)

Goffman first gently spoofs upper middle-class cosmopolitanism, then attacks it more sharply. The 'sophistication' of Hyde Park wives resides in a 'willingness to handle a depicted experience in different ways, and an unwillingness to handle it in the customary way' (1949: 76). The unwillingness of these subjects to be completely bound by certain norms, their 'sophistication', does seem to disturb the Goffman of 1949 who finally adjudges it, in unusually unguarded terms, as part of 'a general trend towards the corruption of single-mindedness' (1949: 77).

Goffman's MA thesis provides a picture of his developing approach to sociology. The TAT conception of projection is inverted and transformed into social form to resurface in his PhD dissertation as the idea of self that is 'projected' in ordinary interaction, one short step from the famous notion of self-presentation. The TAT's dependence on 'the act of make-believe' (1949: 18) speaks to a longer-range general theme of his sociology, how fantasy realms are implicated in 'reality'. Goffman's scepticism towards quantifiable variable analysis in sociological inquiry may have originated in his Toronto days (Spillius 1993). However, these misgivings are given substance through his engagement in empirical research. Goffman's later (1971: xviii) sarcastic and peremptory dismissal of traditional research designs, his suspicion of interview techniques, and his valorization of observational methods, may well be grounded in his 1940s research experiences in Hyde Park, Chicago as he worked toward his first graduate degree.

EARLY PAPERS: CLASS STATUS SYMBOLS, COOLING THE MARK OUT AND THE SERVICE STATION DEALER

The two papers and the commercial report that Goffman published before completing his PhD dissertation in December 1953 provide important insights into his emergent sociological perspective. They address seemingly disparate topics – how class status is displayed, how people adapt to failure, and how service station dealers perceive their work situation – but some common themes run through them. Fraud and deception make an early appearance in Goffman's writings, as becomes evident in the paper 'Symbols of class status' (1951), Goffman's first publication in an academic journal.

Status symbols identify the social capacity to be imputed to a person in 'ordinary communication' and thus how others should treat that person. Unlike collective symbols, which draw persons together irrespective of their differences into a 'single moral community', status symbols serve to 'visibly divide the social world into categories of persons … helping to maintain solidarity within a category and hostility between different categories' (1951: 294). Goffman is fascinated by the possibility that persons may use status symbols falsely to signify a status they do not actually possess. He writes: 'this paper is concerned with the pressures that play upon behaviour as a result of the fact that a symbol of status is not always a very good test of status' (1951: 295). Only then does Goffman restrict his attention to one sub-set of status symbols: class status symbols. The topic, of course, is Warneresque (Goffman acknowledges Warner as providing 'direction' for the study) but the focus on the discrepancy between symbol and actual position is something that would soon be recognized as characteristically Goffman's.

People can pretend to possess an unentitled class status by their misleading use of the appropriate symbols. However, their misrepresentation does not provoke legal sanctions. They 'commit a presumption, not a crime' (1951: 297). This form of presumptuousness does not overwhelm the world because there are a number of 'restrictive devices' (1951: 297–301) limiting the fraudulent use of class status symbols. These include 'moral restrictions', flowing from constraints in the person's conscience, to 'cultivation restrictions', where investments of time and energy are called for (such as playing golf competently). These restrictions tend to operate in clusters, effectively cross-referencing each other. They are manifest at the level of 'ordinary communication'.

Elements of the 1951 paper anticipate subsequent major themes in Goffman's sociology. The term 'self-representation' makes a brief appearance (p. 296) and embryonic versions of the 'working consensus' and the impression management thesis of *The Presentation of Self in Everyday Life* also feature. The risk of a discrepancy between class status symbol and its reality in ordinary communication is later generalized to become an endemic feature of symbol use in face-to-face interaction.

Perhaps Goffman finally discovered he was 'Goffman' with the 1952 publication of 'On cooling the mark out: some aspects of adaptation to failure'. A concern with the fraudulent aspects of social life is again prominent in this paper, where Goffman treats consolation as a social process. Its unusual title derives from Goffman's decision to use the metaphor of the confidence game to unpack features of how people adapt to failure in a job or a relationship. In the confidence game there is a final phase that occurs after the 'operator' has successfully concluded the 'blow off' or 'sting', where the 'mark' is consoled or 'cooled out' about the loss just incurred. The aim of the exercise is to help the mark to come to terms with their foolish loss. The sting can only be successful if the mark does not 'raise a squawk'.

For the first time, the social self is introduced. Adaptation to loss sheds light on the relation 'between involvements and the selves that are involved' (1952: 451). The paper continues Goffman's interest in the disjunctive: here it is not the discrepancy between actual and implied class status but rather the problematic discrepancy between the mark's initial conception of self and the one needing to be cooled out.

The individual, Goffman argues, can acquire a self from any status, role or relationship in which they become involved, and an alteration in the status, role or relationship will bring about an alteration in the person's self-conception (1952: 453). Cooling out is only necessary when the person is involuntarily deprived of a status, role or relationship that reflects unfavourably upon the person, in other words where loss gives rise to humiliation.

Goffman's analysis turns on four general problems about the cooling out process. First, where in society is cooling out called for? It is frequently necessary when someone fails to get a job or a promotion, or where asymmetrical sentiments are expressed towards a friendship, though it can also occur when a customer makes a complaint or when a person faces a dire circumstance like a fatal illness or death sentence. Second, what are the typical ways persons can be cooled out? They include: permitting expressions of anger, offering another chance to qualify and offering an alternative status as a consolation prize. Third, what happens to those who refused to be cooled out? They may 'turn sour' or they may go into competition with the operator. Fourth, how can cooling out be avoided? 'Playing safe' is one tactic here, as is 'two irons in the fire' or maintaining a 'Plan B'.

What light does the analysis of cooling out shed on the nature of the self in society? First of all Goffman presents conclusions about the 'structure of persons':

> a person is an individual who becomes involved in a value of some
> kind – a role, a status, a relationship, an ideology – and then makes
> a public claim that he is to be defined and treated as someone who
> possesses the value or property in question. (1952: 461)

When the person lays claim to a self, it must be consonant with 'the objective facts of his social life'. However, Goffman acknowledges that there is room for 'sympathetic interpretation' of the 'facts' that can sustain a viable self. The rudiments of the dramaturgical self are present. However Goffman has yet to restrict his analytic focus to the sphere of face-to-face interaction.

Second, the presence of cooling out procedures has general implications about the nature of persons and their activities. It highlights the existence of a norm that urges persons 'to keep their chins up and make the best of it – a sort of social sanitation enjoining torn and tattered persons to keep themselves packaged up' (p. 461). Furthermore, that persons can 'sustain these profound embarrassments implies a certain looseness and lack of interpenetration in the organization of his several life-activities' (p. 461). Often the person who fails in one role (e.g. at work) may succeed in another (e.g. in their marriage). However, if the failure spreads over several roles, then the psychotherapist, 'society's cooler', will need to be called in.

Goffman ends by recognizing that he has dealt only with the 'sugar coating' of adaptation to failure and not the bitter pill of failure itself. Those who have 'failed' – been sacked, divorced, or found guilty – have in one sense become socially 'dead'. Some of the socially dead are sifted into jails, mental institutions, old people's homes, hobo jungles and the like, but there are many situations in life where the socially dead and the successful coexist. It is in this sense that 'the dead are sorted but not segregated and continue to walk among the living' (1952: 463).

The style of the paper is distinctively Goffmanesque. It is the first place in which Goffman consciously applies metaphor as a methodological device. It showcases his already subtle grasp of Kenneth Burke's method of 'perspective by incongruity' – the juxtaposing of incongruous ideas to yield new insight. Goffman's exuberance with this new found device is everywhere evident: arresting comparisons and witticisms tumble out of almost every page. Goffman appears to have found his true *metier*.

The February 1953 report, 'The service station dealer: the man and his work' (Goffman 1953b), casts some interesting sidelights on Goffman the occupational ethnographer. Commissioned by Social Research Inc. (SRI), a firm Lloyd Warner established in 1946 with former students William Henry and Burleigh Gardner, this is a study of the men (bear in mind it is the early 1950s) who manage petrol stations in Chicago. SRI took market research beyond its conventional survey basis, drawing upon anthropological, psychological and sociological techniques to explore the motivational dimensions of consumption (Levy 2003; Warner 1988). Goffman was just one of many graduate students employed by SRI to undertake a commercially useful research project. The report was prepared for the American Petroleum Institute, a body founded in 1919 to represent oil business interests in the USA. Approximately 100 pages long (including interview and social data schedules), the report examines the attitudes of service station dealers to the work they do and the companies and industry they represent.

Goffman's involvement is easy enough to comprehend, since Warner and Henry were his dissertation advisors. Goffman seeks to discover 'what kind of men are running service stations, how they behave and what their attitudes are' (1953b: 1). To furnish answers to these questions, Goffman draws on interviews with 204 dealers at various locations across the Chicago area. Open-ended interview sessions examined in depth what the men felt about their work, their customers their status and the oil companies who leased them the service stations. SRI's general approach sought to elucidate the men's views in a psychologically subtler and more ethnographically sensitive manner than questionnaires allowed. Light was shed on the dealer's personality through the TAT (a particular specialism of Henry's) and detailed 'social data' were collected to pin down social class location (Warner's preoccupation). But perhaps the most striking aspect of the report is the hidden hand of another of Goffman's teachers, Everett C. Hughes (Jaworski 2000).

The report can be read as a detailed application and instantiation of themes from Hughes' (1945) study of the dilemmas and contradictions to which persons are exposed in particular roles and statuses (as a commercial report, there are no references to academic sources, and many details about method are omitted). Goffman suggests that three aspects of the dealer's occupational role produce difficulties: he is seen as part businessman, part servant-attendant and part technician. He has to manage the station and enjoys the independence and status that goes with business activities. Yet he is also called on to perform menial services, wiping customers' windshields or removing dirty objects from the car. Sometimes, too, he is expected to possess some mechanical expertise. The contradictory social definitions and demands linked to each of these aspects of the dealer's role lead to tensions and difficulties that the body of the report examines.

Goffman begins with 'individual adjustments' to the occupation, identifying the characteristics of three types of energetic and accomplished dealers and two types of apathetic and erratic types. He then examines the dealer's work situation, beginning with relations with customers. Goffman draws out what, from the dealer's point of view, makes a 'good' and 'bad' customer. He suggests that some dealers 'train' their customers to joke and exchange in pleasantries, so that they can extract a 'social living' (p. 32) from customers as well as an economic one. Some service station dealers also build up a clientele for their business by being pointedly courteous and smiling, recognizing regular customers, adopting a sincere and enthusiastic manner and by being generally disciplined in their responses to customers (pp. 45–9). Work is not merely done, but done in a stylised manner. Dealers frequently see themselves as persons without pretensions, which makes for relaxed and often joking relationships with employees. However, the perception that dealers are not socially distant from their employees makes their acceptance into local business communities difficult.

The dealer is isolated from other business people and also has a remote relationship with the company. The dealer's main point of contact is the truck driver who delivers a new consignment of gas every few weeks. Goffman quotes one dealer who likens his relationship to the company to that of the 'stepchild' – 'they are only concerned if you don't cooperate, then they throw you out' (pp. 61, 73). If dealers are indifferent towards the company then that is because they have the attitudes and feelings characteristic of small businessmen but find themselves in a situation where big business is coming to dominate their corner of the economy. Successful dealers learn to handle these vicissitudes by cultivating a clientele while less competent dealers 'feel confused and uncertain, they seek a shelter, a benevolent protector, which the system does not provide. And naturally they react with complaints and hostility directed both at the company and at their competitors' (p. 76). Service station dealers, Goffman concludes, work hard and conscientiously but the vagaries of their work situation – the many dilemmas and contradictions of their occupational status – mean that 'they do not communicate a pride or enthusiasm that would "sell" the public on the industry' (1953b: 78).

COMMUNICATION CONDUCT IN AN ISLAND COMMUNITY

Goffman's doctoral dissertation, submitted to the Department of Sociology at the University of Chicago in December 1953, was the product of 12 months' fieldwork carried out in the Shetland Isles between December 1949 and May 1951. It repays close study because it represents the first, fully-fledged statement of his sociological thought. Unlike his earlier work, the focus of investigative attention falls firmly on face-to-face interaction. It is not a conventional community study but a study of 'conversational interaction' *in* one community that he hoped would contribute towards the construction of 'a systematic framework useful in studying interaction throughout our society' (Goffman 1953: 1). In some respects the doctoral dissertation is a defensive document. In it Goffman tones down his inventive use of metaphor in order to convey clearly to his examiners his core ideas about the interaction order.

Goffman's research in Unst was facilitated by Lloyd Warner, who received an invitation from Ralph Piddington, an acquaintance from his days in Australia with Radcliffe-Brown. A new Department of Social Anthropology had been established at the University of Edinburgh in 1946 and Piddington wanted a good doctoral student who could help galvanize the new structure (Winkin 1988: 51–2). Warner suggested Goffman, who began work at the University of Edinburgh in October 1949. From the start, the Edinburgh department resisted narrow disciplinary compartmentalization and it encouraged anthropological investigations of the anthropologist's own society. Although 'anthropology at home' is now a popular approach, it was far less common in the late 1940s. Goffman's mentor, W. Lloyd Warner, was an early exponent of the approach. He conducted fieldwork among the Murngin in Australia then applied the same techniques of research to analyse American communities (the famous 'Yankee City' studies of the 1940s).

In seeking to construct a systematic framework for the study of conversational interaction, Goffman employed the usual anthropological technique of ethnography, but he stressed that his aim was primarily systematic, not ethnographic: the dissertation is *not* an ethnography of the Shetland Isle community. He confines his interest to the characteristics of interactional practices. Questions about the frequency, intensity, history and functions of these practices, proper as they are, are set outside the dissertation's remit.

Goffman describes his fieldwork role thus:

> I settled down in the community as an American college student interested in gaining firsthand experience in the economics of island farming. Within these limits I tried to play an unexceptional and acceptable role in community life. My real aim was to be an observant participant, rather than a participating observer. (1953a: 2)

Goffman participated in a wide range of activities, such as meals, work, schooling, shopping, weddings, parties, and funerals. He was able to study more intensively three settings in which he was a regular participant: village socials, games of billiards and hotel life. He experienced hotel life both as a guest and as 'second dishwasher' during busy periods. In the early months of the study he was able to take notes in the course of the events he was witnessing, but later found himself in situations where note-taking would have been regarded as improper and so the recording of observations had to wait until the end of the day. Systematic interviewing was not undertaken, but some interviews were conducted on matters which 'the islanders felt were proper subjects for interviews' (1953a: 5).

The study took place in Baltasound ('Dixon' in the dissertation), a village of approximately 100 households. The main class cleavage was between the 'gentry' (numbering two families in Dixon) and the 'locals' or 'commoner' class (p. 17). Goffman concentrated his observational work on the social evenings in the village hall, the games of billiards held in an adjoining annex, and at the hotel. The social evenings were held in Dixon's community hall every fortnight between September and March. At 8 p.m. the 'planned entertainment' (usually whist, although sometimes a concert or auction) would begin and continue until around

11 p.m. when tea and buns were served. After this intermission a dance was held which often continued to 2.30 in the morning. The socials served as the focal point of the social life of many islanders and were generally well attended. Billiards, played in the reading room of the community hall, attracted a narrower group of the Dixon population, chiefly men aged 25–35 and 50–65. Here the business of the community could be conducted in informal conditions; solidarity between the younger and older generation was forged and older community leaders were afforded the opportunity to train the upcoming generation. Possibly the most memorable illustrations from the Shetland fieldwork stem from the hotel where Goffman stayed and worked. The young women considered the 'leading belles' of Dixon customarily worked in the hotel in the summer months. The hotel attracted a middle- and upper-class clientele and served 'as a centre of diffusion of higher class British values' (p. 30) among the predominantly lower-class inhabitants of Dixon. It is noteworthy that Goffman concentrates on these public or semi-public settings. He lived on his own, did not participate in family life and was only involved on the fringes of economic activities. Goffman lived in a community but was not of it. For his rather definite analytic purposes, this may not have mattered much.

Conversational interaction, Goffman announces on p. 1 of his dissertation, is 'one species of social order'. Consequently, the first analytical chapter of the dissertation sets out a model of social order derived from Talcott Parsons' *The Social System* (1951) and especially Chester I. Barnard's *The Functions of the Executive* (1947). Goffman's procedure is to articulate a general model of social order in nine propositions, applying each in turn to the phenomenon of conversational interaction. He shows how ideas originally developed to handle institutional issues can shed light on the characteristics of conversational interaction. What then does it mean to suggest that conversational interaction is a social order? Goffman's nine claims (1953a: 33–8) can be summarized as follows.

1 The social order of conversational interaction is produced by different participants exchanging communicative acts, i.e. a flow of messages. One participant's message becomes the starting point of the next participant's message. The different acts of each participant are integrated into a continuous and uninterrupted exchange of messages, the 'work flow of conversational interaction'.

2 The communicative acts of the participant are bound by the legitimate expectations of other participants. These expectations limit how the participant is likely to behave, and they have a moral right to expect him to behave within these limits.

3 'Proper contribution from participants is assured or "motivated" by means of a set of positive sanctions or rewards and negative or punishments' (p. 34). The characteristic feature of the social order of conversational interaction is that it is enforced by sanctions that can be immediately expressed, i.e. moral approval and disapproval articulated in the course of interaction, rather than by more distant instrumental sanctions (fines, imprisonment, etc.).

4 'Any concrete social order must occur within a wider social context. The flow of action between the order and its social environment must come under regulation that is integrated into the order as such' (p. 35). This feature can be applied directly to conversational interaction. It provides a source of Goffman's core image of the interaction order as relatively autonomous of other kinds of social order to which it is nonetheless linked.

5 'When the rules are not adhered to, or when no rules seem applicable, participants cease to know how to behave or what to expect from others. At the social level, the integration of the participant's actions breaks down and we have social disorganization or social disorder. At the same time, the participants suffer personal disorganization and anomie' (p. 35). In conversational interaction such disorganization is manifest as embarrassment that for participants introduces a momentary disorientation and a sense of flustering or confusion.

6 'A person who breaks rules is an offender; his breaking them is an offense. He who breaks rules continuously is a deviant' (p. 35). Applied to conversational interaction, offenders can be described as *gauche* or out of place. Their offences (i.e. acts causing embarrassment) can be described as *gaffes, faux pas* and indiscretions. In the ways these offences contrast with the orderliness ordinarily expected in conversational interaction, they serve to highlight the requirements for interaction to run smoothly. Those who persistently deviate in this way can be called 'faulty persons'.

7 'When a rule is broken, the offender ought to feel guilty or remorseful, and the offended ought to feel righteously indignant' (p. 36). In conversational interaction, the offender's guilt is felt as shame. The offended are entitled to feel shocked or affronted.

8 'An offense to or infraction of the social order calls forth emergency correctives which re-establish the threatened order, compensating for the damage done to it. These compensatory actions will tend to reinstate not only the work flow but also the moral norms which regulated it' (1953a: 36). Although offended participants in conversational interaction can ignore the offender, it is more usual for them to respond in an attitude of tolerance and forbearance, giving rise to a 'working

acceptance' maintained by the employment of 'protective strategies' and 'corrective strategies'.

9 'Given the rules of the social order, we find that individual participants develop ruses and tricks for achieving private ends that are proscribed by the rules, in such a way as not to break the rules' (p. 38). In conversational interaction private ends are sought through scarcely noticeable 'gain strategies' that alter the working acceptance just enough to suit the individual's wishes.

The social order model establishes for Goffman the sociological legitimacy of his chosen field of investigation. However, the model does not sufficiently emphasize the forbearant maintenance of the working acceptance, which Goffman regards as the crucial characteristic of conversational interaction. That a participant is required to be forbearant implies feelings of hostility or resentment towards the person who must be forbearingly accepted. It also implies a potential discrepancy between the participant's 'real' feelings and those shown towards other participants. Goffman acknowledges that the psychology of forbearance can be quite complex. However, offences against the social order of conversation are so frequent and gain strategies so common that:

> it is often better to conceive of interaction not as a scene of harmony but as an arrangement for pursuing a cold war. A working acceptance may thus be likened to a temporary truce, a *modus vivendi* for carrying on negotiations and vital business. (1953a: 40)

A forbearant outlook is thus constantly required and the working consensus that results is 'one of the few general bases of real consensus between persons' (p. 40).

By treating conversational interaction as a species of social order Goffman succeeds in placing its study squarely within sociology. Goffman indicates how the orderliness of conversational interaction is produced in actual instances by the practices of the participants. Equally, conversational interaction's order can be threatened through these same practices.

The remainder of the dissertation falls into three decreasingly abstract parts, beginning with an analysis of information about one's self. In a chapter anticipating the Introduction to *The Presentation of Self in Everyday Life,* the characteristics of linguistic and expressive behaviour are contrasted and the role of each in the management of information about oneself examined. Ichheiser's (1949) observation that the expression of one person becomes the impression that the other acquires of the person is introduced. The differing communication consequences of linguistic and expressive messages are emphasized. An expressive message is taken rather than sent, conveyed rather than communicated, and the recipient plays a more active role than the sender. Since recipients will scrutinize both linguistic and expressive messages in the furtherance of their ends, senders will tend to exert 'tactical control' (p. 74) over both types of message. However recipients are favoured by a communicative asymmetry: senders can more successfully control linguistic than expressive messages. A 'game of concealment and search' (p. 84) emerges where the recipient has the advantage in discovering facts about the individual. While expressive behaviour is usually considered to be involuntary and calculated, Goffman notes the possibility that it may be modified by the sender 'with malice aforethought' and concludes that 'a very complex dialectic is in progress' (p. 87).

An important qualification of this emphasis on calculative elements in the control of information about one's self is given in Goffman's discussion of 'sign situations'. These are situations where an irrelevant, improper or incorrect evaluation is conveyed and tension arises in the interaction. In such situations 'diplomatic labor' (p. 102) is required of the participants to rectify the impression conveyed. Sign situations indicate the need for participants to exercise some responsibility for the impressions they provide to ensure that these impressions are not offensive to recipients. Thus, conversational interaction generates problems of ritual management as well as informational management. Weber and G.H. Mead emphasized that people take each other's actions into consideration (in pursuit of personal ends) without giving corresponding attention to how people give consideration to others. Goffman concludes:

> the best model for an object to which we give consideration is not a person at all, but a sacred idol, image, or god. It is to such sacred objects that we show in extreme what we show to persons. We feel that these objects possess some sacred value, whether positive and purifying, or negative and polluting, and we feel disposed to perform rites before these objects. These rites we perform as frequently and compulsively as the sacred value of the object is great. These worshipful acts express our adoration, or fear, or hate, and serve for the idol as periodic assurances that we are keeping faith and deserve to be in its favor. When in the idol's immediate presence we act with ritual care, appreciating that pious actions may favorably dispose the idol toward us and that impious actions may anger the idol and cause it to perform angry actions against us. Persons, unless they are of high office, do not have as much sacred power or *mana* as do idols, and hence need not be trusted with as much ceremony. An idol is to a person as a rite is to etiquette. (1953a: 104)

From the very outset, Goffman's sociology has a place for considerateness as well as calculation.

Goffman next presents his basic terminology for the analysis of this species of social order, including 'social occasion', 'interplay' (a precursor of 'encounter'), 'accredited participation', and 'safe supplies'. Although some of these concepts appear in Goffman's later published work in modified form, it is noteworthy that many of his central ideas about the organization of interaction had already crystallized. It is possible to read all Goffman's publications on interaction in the following decade as enlarging, refining and filling in the small print of ideas first set out in his 1953 PhD.

The last part of the dissertation, 'Conduct during interplay' opens with an important distinction between euphoric and dysphoric interplay. In dysphoric interplay participants 'feel ill at ease', out of countenance, non-plussed, self-conscious, embarrassed or out of place because of the sheer presence of others or because of the actions of others (p. 243). When these conditions are absent from the interplay it can be described as euphoric. Despite the psychological language in which the distinction is couched, Goffman maintains that euphoria and dysphoria are features of interplay, not participants' feelings (pp. 246–7). Thus personally distressing information can be conveyed in euphoric interplay and good news conveyed in a way that leaves the participant feeling embarrassed. How euphoric interplay is possible is a major concern of the last part of Goffman's dissertation.

The key is the nature of the participant's involvement in interplay. Euphoric interplay will result when participants show the kind of involvement proper to the interplay in question. To show too little or too much involvement is likely to generate dysphoria. A state of proper involvement, Goffman (p. 257) concludes, requires a little bending of the rules of tact. This state lies between the boredom engendered by fully following the rules of tact and the embarrassment that occurs when these rules are broken.

Spontaneous involvement is thus the desired state of involvement in interplay. But some persons seem to be chronically incapable of routinely achieving this state. These Goffman labels 'faulty persons'; they 'bring offense and dysphoria to almost every interplay in which they participate, causing others to feel ill at ease whether or not the offenders themselves are embarrassed' (p. 260). Faulty persons highlight the importance of how one handles oneself during interplay: 'poise' (p. 275).

Participants project a certain definition of themselves and other participants by every word and gesture they make. These definitions, together with whatever participants know about each other and the appropriate responses to given categories of person and symbols of status, constitute for Goffman 'a preliminary state of social information' (p. 300) for the interplay. Participants will usually seek to validate these initial understandings. Thus interplay tends to be 'an inherently conservative thing' (p. 301) in which participants will merely elaborate and modify the initial understandings. Sometimes, however, something may be communicated during the course of an interplay that discredits the self projected through the initial definition of the situation. This represents a threat to the working acceptance.

To avoid or remedy such threats, protective and corrective strategies are employed. Goffman discusses at length (pp. 329–42) the role of discretion, hedging, politeness, unseriousness, sang-froid, feigned indifference and non-observance of the disruptive incident. These strategies are important for the management of projected selves in interplay.

In the concluding chapter Goffman introduces the term 'the interaction order' that posthumously became the leading characterization of his sociology's focal concern. (It is curious that Goffman did not use this apt label earlier to describe his central interest, for as he recognized, alternatives such as the study of 'public life' or 'public order' are much more unsatisfactory; see Goffman 1963a: 8–9; 1971: xi, n.1.) The interaction order organizes the communicative conduct of persons in face-to-face interaction. In 1953 Goffman saw the interaction order as a very basic social order, though neither then nor later did he make grand claims for its primacy either to sociologists or participants. In the concluding chapter Goffman writes:

> In this study I have attempted to abstract from diverse comings-together in Dixon the orderliness that is common to all of them, the orderliness that obtains by virtue of the fact that those present are engaged in spoken communication. All instances of engagement-in-speech are seen as members of a single class of events, each of which exhibits the same kind of social order, giving rise to the same kind of social organization in response to the same kind of normative structure and the same kind of social control. Regardless of the specific roles and capacities which an individual employs when he engages in interaction, he must in addition take the role of communicator and participant; regardless of the particular content of the spoken communication, order must prevail in the flow of messages by which the content is conveyed. (1953a: 345)

INFLUENCES

Goffman is frequently characterized as a leading exponent of symbolic interactionism. As he observed in interview, it was a label that applied as well to him as anyone, but it was too vague a characterization of social life to provide his sociology with much guidance. Certainly, Goffman was 'sympathetic' to Herbert Blumer's writings on concepts and method (Verhoeven 1993: 320). But in graduate school he apparently had infrequent contact with Blumer. As this chapter's review of Goffman's early work shows, there is very little that directly connects it to Blumer's approach.

A surer method of tracking formative influences on Goffman is to consider the training and interests of his two key teachers, Everett Hughes and Lloyd Warner. Seen in the genealogical terms commonly used to trace intellectual influence, Goffman is a third generation descendant of Georg Simmel and Emile Durkheim. It was the first Chicago school's founding figure, Robert E. Park, whose 'only formal instruction in sociology', he later recalled, came from listening to Simmel's lectures at Berlin, who ensured Simmel a lasting place in the sociology syllabi at Chicago. One of Park's students, Everett C. Hughes, passed the Simmel torch to the postwar generation. It was Hughes whom Goffman considered his most important teacher at Chicago. Of course, Hughes did more than alert Goffman to the significance of Simmel's work (Jaworski 2000). From Hughes Goffman also learned the importance of rudiments of observational fieldwork and once characterized his own approach as a marriage of Hughesian urban ethnography to G.H. Mead's social psychology (Verhoeven 1993). But from Simmel's example Goffman would have seen the cogency of an associational conception of society and the importance of a formal sociology that abstracted the general forms of social life from their particular contents. Goffman prefaced his PhD dissertation with a long excerpt about the 'immeasurable number of less conspicuous forms of relationship and kinds of interaction … (that) incessantly tie men together' (Simmel 1950: 9–10). In the Preface to *The Presentation of Self in Everyday Life*, Goffman remarks that the justification for his approach is the same as Simmel's. Especially at the level of method, Goffman pursues a Simmelian formal sociology (Smith 1994). As a formal sociologist Goffman aimed to elucidate and analyse a variety of forms of the interaction order, such as the basic kinds of face-work, the forms of alienation from interaction, or the stages of remedial interchange.

Lloyd Warner advised both Goffman's master's thesis and doctoral dissertation, and hired him to write the service station dealers' report. Warner became a protégé of A.R. Radcliffe-Brown while fieldworking in Australia in the late 1920s and absorbed the Durkheimian perspective he championed. The influence of Durkheim is quite explicit in Goffman's ritual model of interaction. It is more diffusely evident in Goffman's remarkable capacity to seek out and name new dimensions of social regulation in interactional conduct. Just as Durkheim demonstrated the social determinants of the apparently personal act of suicide, Goffman showed how many of our seemingly insignificant and idiosyncratic concerns (our expletives when we drop a glass, our discomfort when a stranger on a street holds a glance at us too long) are consequences of the normative ordering of interactional conduct. Goffman the Durkheim revisionist is never more clearly present than when he is drawing our attention to the social sources of a feeling or item of conduct we had thought uniquely ours.

These lineage lines contextualize Goffman's sociology but do not explain its unique shape and preoccupations. Later Goffman would grow exasperated by critics who sought to label – and thus assimilate – his ideas to sociology's major paradigms. In his view sociological traditions were there to be creatively developed, applied and modified, not slavishly followed. This chapter has traced the formation of Goffman's sociological approach, which was almost fully in place by the completion of his doctoral dissertation in 1953. The University of Chicago proved to be the crucible in which a number of critical influences were condensed into the distinctive approach now instantly recognizable as 'Goffman's sociology'.

3
Interaction's Orderliness

> Encounters are everywhere, but it is difficult to describe sociologically the stuff they are made of.
>
> (Goffman 1961b: 19)

Goffman was unparalleled in sociologically explicating the constituent elements of the interaction order. Yet nowhere did he offer a consolidated statement of what his sociology of the interaction order had achieved. The posthumously published, 'The interaction order', might have been hoped to provide a conclusive theoretical integration. In the event, the last paper that he knew would be published did give a sketch of interaction's basic units, structures and processes. It was an all-too-brief account, however, only cursorily connected to his more substantial writings. Goffman's analytic frameworks manifest clear systematic intent, without any apparent wish to build a system. Goffman's ideas seem to be continually in process, reaching no final resting place. The difficulties for any commentator seeking to specify the key elements of the sociology of the interaction order are obvious, part of a more general criticism of Goffman's method (see Chapter 8). However, it would be a mistake to suppose that Goffman's ideas about interaction did not cumulate or lacked a systematic basis. Certain terms and themes recur throughout Goffman's writings. In these terms and themes we can locate the central topics and preoccupations of Goffman's sociology of the interaction order. These are: a general social psychology of interactional expressivity; a set of basic concepts of co-presence; and extended recourse to theatrical, game and ritual metaphors as analytic devices to sociologically illuminate features of the interaction order.

Goffman's sociology of interaction rests upon some very general social psychological presuppositions about the nature of human expressivity in face-to-face interaction. These presuppositions allow Goffman to set out the elemental concepts of co-presence needed to understand the interaction order's basic architecture. The concepts of co-presence underpin the detailed sociological analysis of interaction achieved through an imaginative mobilization of the metaphors of drama, game and ritual. The dramaturgical metaphor is the vehicle for Goffman's fascination with the performed and displayed aspects of social interaction. Dramaturgy is not synonymous with Goffman's entire sociology, as is sometimes assumed, but it does capture his abiding preoccupation with the enacted character of social life and in particular his interest in how interactional performances can fall flat. The game metaphor is mobilized to highlight how persons can influence the impressions others have of them through the management and control of personal information. The game metaphor highlights the designed, calculated aspects of interactional conduct. Ritual, the third principal metaphor, applies aspects of Durkheim's sociology of religion to everyday interactional conduct. The ritual metaphor articulates the basic forms of regard and respect for both the other and oneself that can be conveyed interactionally. These metaphors figure in different combinations in Goffman's writings, providing the major analytic resources deployed by Goffman in his exploration of the interaction order.

In Goffman's efforts to systematically uncover the sources of interaction's orderliness – his attempt to develop an interactional syntax – the dissertation approved in 1953 was just the beginning. Building on the dissertation's ideas, he published four important essays ('On face-work' (1955a); 'The nature of deference and demeanor' (1956c); 'Embarrassment and social organization' (1956b) and 'Alienation from interaction' (1957a)) and the first edition of *The Presentation of Self in Everyday Life* (1956a) in the following four years. He consolidated his interaction sociology as a Berkeley professor in the decade from 1958, producing *Encounters* (1961b), *Behavior in Public Places* (1963a), *Interaction Ritual* (1967) (which reprinted the mid-1950s essays together with a new one, 'Where the action is'), and *Strategic Interaction* (1969). In these works Goffman concentrates attention on practices of interaction, endeavouring to identify the rules that largely lie outside of our awareness and to specify the structures (or forms or 'units') we take for granted in everyday interaction. The pursuit of the interactional systematics also occupied Goffman's later writings, notably *Relations in Public* (1971) and *Gender Advertisements* (1979). However, it is the earlier work that establishes the key constituents of Goffman's sociology of interaction.

SOCIAL PSYCHOLOGICAL PRESUPPOSITIONS: EXPRESSIVITY AND ITS CONSEQUENCES

George Herbert Mead's (1934) contention that taking the attitude or role of the other is a fundamental feature of human social life was very fully absorbed by Goffman. Mead saw that the capacity to take the attitude of the other – to look at things from the standpoint of the other – was the key to understanding how the self developed. Goffman in effect asks: how does co-presence bear on the process of taking the attitude of the other? His solution centres on the 'expressions' that convey information to others about the individual.

The body-to-body starting point of his sociological project requires some presuppositions about human psychology and embodiment. There is 'an inevitable psychobiological element' (1983a: 3) in face-to-face interaction because emotion, cognition and muscular effort are intrinsic to its accomplishment. The psychobiological properties in question are set out in the 'necessarily abstract' Introduction of *Presentation of Self* that Goffman invites readers to 'skip' (and are elaborated in Goffman 1963a: 13–17 and 1969a: 4–10). Four ideas recur in the general social psychology of the interactant that Goffman synthesized from Adam Smith, Charles Cooley, G.H. Mead and Gustav Ichheiser.

First, in interaction the *expressiveness* of the person is the medium through which information about the individual – their status, mood, intentions, competence, etc. – is conveyed to others. In his dissertation Goffman wrote:

In the style of the act, in the manner in which the act is performed, in the relation of the act to the context in which it occurs – in all these ways something about the actor is presented in the character of his act. The tendency for the character of the actor to overflow into the character of his acts is usually called the expressive aspect of behavior. (1953a: 50)

In face-to-face interaction, when we *express* ourselves through a well-turned phrase, a tone of voice, a look of the eyes, or a posture, we *impress* others present in a certain way (1959: 2).

Second, information about the individual is conveyed in interaction through *expressive messages* 'given' and 'given off'. The information communicated through a speaker's talk is the primary example of an expression given. The tone of the speaker's talk and the accompanying posture, facial gestures and so forth that the speaker exudes are examples of expressions given off. Expressions we give are taken to be intended; those we give off are often assumed to be unintentional.

Third, expressions given and given off in interaction provide a *flow of information* rich in qualifiers. Each individual is accessible to the ordinary (or 'naked') senses of all the others present, and they to him/her. Expressive information is (a) reflexive i.e. conveyed by the very person it is about and (b) embodied i.e. evinced by the person's bodily signs. Individuals draw inferences about others' conduct by 'auditing' or 'monitoring' the expressive information they convey.

Fourth, the fact of co-presence facilitates *opportunities for feedback*, which can make the monitoring process complex. Interactants occupy symmetrical roles as 'transceivers' of expressive information: 'each giver is himself a receiver, and each receiver a giver' (1963a: 16). Thus a 'special mutuality' arises when persons are co-present. Each interactant can gauge the other's actions and adjust their own actions accordingly, in the knowledge that the other may already be anticipating this adjustment. This special mutuality can assist the revelation of interactants' intentions and purposes, but it can just as easily be used to conceal them through blocking or misdirection. The special mutuality of co-presence locks the interactant into an 'intelligently helpful and hindering world' (1963a: 16). Goffman shows the complexity of taking the attitude of the other in the interaction order.

CONCEPTUALIZING CO-PRESENCE

The term 'interaction' is often indiscriminately used. Goffman makes significant inroads toward clarification with the important conceptual trilogy of 'social gathering', 'social situation', 'social occasion'. These concepts identify different dimensions of co-presence. They provide a stable conceptual core to a sociological project that was remarkably consistent yet neither linear nor straightforwardly cumulative (Williams 1980).

A *social gathering* is when two or more persons find themselves in one another's immediate presence. Goffman reserves the term *social situation* to refer to the spatial environment of 'mutual monitoring possibilities' available to the co-present persons of a gathering. A social situation arises when two or more people find themselves in each other's physical presence, thereby allowing mutual monitoring of one another; it ends when the next-to-last participant leaves (1963a: 18). The concept of social situation draws attention to the shaping of conduct by the fact of co-presence. The same act of the solitary individual – for example, a moment spent gazing vacantly out of the window – can be transformed when it is performed in a social situation such as an interview. The *social occasion* is the wider social entity, such as a farewell party or a day at the office, within which gatherings and situations take place. The social occasion is whatever it is that has brought together this group of people to this particular time and place. This more diffuse concept indicates that situations and gatherings do not float freely but are linked to and structured by broader sources of social regulation.

Having revealed some different species of human co-presence commonly concealed by the generic term, 'interaction', Goffman returns to the key 'unit', the social gathering. Two polar types of gathering, unfocused and focused, are distinguished. The communicative behaviour of co-present persons can be thought of in terms of 'two steps'. The first step, *unfocused interaction*, occurs between those who come together in a social situation while pursuing their own lines of concern. People walking down a street or quietly sitting in a waiting room provide examples of unfocused gatherings. The second step, *focused interaction*, takes place when those co-present 'openly cooperate to sustain a single focus of attention' (1963a: 24), as in a conversation, a board game, or a joint task carried out by a close circle of contributors. The 'focused gathering' that results is also called a 'face engagement', or 'encounter' or 'situated activity system'.

The rules that govern and regulate situations and gatherings Goffman calls 'situational proprieties'. These rules make up a moral code that is distinct from the better-known codes that govern personal relationships or professional life.

Situational proprieties include the 'common courtesies' and culturally-learned, practical knowledge about posture, spatial arrangements, tone of voice and so forth appropriate to a situation. Perhaps the most general situational propriety of all, Goffman surmises, is 'the rule obliging participants to "fit in"' (1963a: 11) i.e. to 'be good' and 'not make a scene'. This is not an endorsement of social conformity. Goffman insists that situational proprieties are not universally and unconditionally binding on the interactant. Anticipating ethnomethodological notions of rule-use, Goffman maintains that for the interactant, rules are matters to 'be taken into consideration, whether as something to follow or to carefully circumvent' (1963a: 42). Later, he suggests that rules are 'enabling conventions' (1983a: 5) that establish a backdrop of common expectations against which all upcoming actions can be adjudged as, for example, a friendly wave or an intimidating remark. Situational proprieties imply situationally sensitive interactants.

Unfocused interaction transpires between unacquainted persons in public places. We do not know these persons, but we are able to make inferences about them on the basis of what they look like and how they are acting. In other words, Goffman suggests, our conjectures about unacquainted persons are made through their 'body idiom' and observable 'involvements'.

Body idiom is the shared vocabulary or 'conventionalized discourse' that enables us to make widely agreed sense about dress, physical gestures such as nodding or waving, facial gestures and the like. Goffman is at pains to distance body idiom from the commoner notion of 'non-verbal language'. The information communicated by expressions given off lacks the symbolic complexity that linguists ascribe to spoken and written language. There is no time out from body idiom in any social encounter, for although 'an individual can stop talking, he cannot stop communicating through body idiom; he must say either the right thing or the wrong thing. He cannot say nothing' (Goffman 1963a: 35).

Involvement is the key to Goffman's early analysis of unfocused interaction. Involvement is 'the capacity of the individual to give, or withhold from giving, concerted attention to some activity at hand – a solitary task, a conversation, a collaborative work effort' (1963a: 43). Goffman then adds: 'involvement in an activity is taken to express the purpose or aim of the actor'. Two pairs of distinctions are sketched. A 'main involvement' takes up most of the individual's attention while a 'side involvement' is whatever else can be carried on without threatening the main involvement (e.g. listening to the radio while assembling a bookcase). The main/side involvement distinction is about what the individual chooses to attend to in carrying out activity. However the second distinction, between 'dominant' and 'subordinate' involvements, concerns the 'claims upon an individual the social occasion obliges him to be ready to recognize'. A 'dominant involvement' is the official business a social occasion requires the individual to recognize, such as a work task (e.g. selling drinks at a station kiosk). Supervisors may tolerate a 'subordinate involvement' (such as checking one's text messages in the gaps between customers arriving to be served) only so long as it does not interfere with the dominant involvement.

While involvement is clearly a 'psychobiological' matter, it also has a social dimension, since the assessment of involvement can only be done on the basis of outward expressions. Appropriate involvement, Goffman emphasizes, depends upon the social occasion and situation. This leads him to speak of 'involvement obligations'. Checking one's text messages when customers are waiting may become a sanctionable matter.

Involvement centres on the situationally appropriate distribution of the individual's attention. In unfocused gatherings, such as busy city streets, the primary principle at work is 'civil inattention' (1963a: 84–85). In Goffman's initial description, passers by size each other up as they approach and then glance downward in a show memorably likened to passing vehicles dipping their lights. Goffman emphasizes the delicate nuancing of acts that display civil inattention, characterizing them as 'the slightest of interpersonal rituals' (1963a: 84) that express that 'one has no untoward intent nor expects to be an object of it' (1977: 327). On the basis of her field research in urban spaces, Lyn Lofland (1998: 30) proposes that civil inattention is 'the sine qua non of city life' that 'makes possible co-presence without commingling, awareness without engrossment, courtesy without conversation'. Yet for some categories of person, civil inattention seems most frequently honoured in the breach. Gardner (1995) recasts Goffman's argument to acknowledge women's 'normalized distaste of public places', and to show how women in public are harassed through such everyday devices as 'street remarks' and requests for 'public aid'.

Goffman's analysis of unfocused interaction was groundbreaking. He disabused us of the notion that public places like streets and parks were an asocial void. His demonstration of its intricate organization by unseen, largely taken-for-granted situational proprieties marked a major advance in our understanding of the public realm (Cahill 1994; Lofland 1998). In *Relations in Public* Goffman further develops the sociology of unfocused interaction with important concepts like 'vehicular unit', a shell controlled by a human pilot which encompasses both pedestrians and vehicles as ordinarily understood, and a 'participation unit', which is not explicitly defined (but see 1963a: 91) and which consists of a subset of the 'single', the unaccompanied person in a public place, and the 'with', the person in the company of one or more others. Aspects of personal territory are analysed under the heading, the 'territories of the self'. 'Tie signs' considers how we can glean evidence of a relationship between unacquainted persons through their 'body placement, posture, gesture, and vocal expression' (1971: 195). Handholding, sharing the same cup or bottle of suntan lotion, and replying to another with a term of endearment are all signs of a particular 'tie' or relationship between persons. In public places persons will constantly check their immediate surround, their *Umwelt* in order to ensure that nothing out of the ordinary is taking place, that 'normal appearances' are being sustained.

In moving from unfocused gatherings to the focused kind, the question arises: how can an encounter be initiated? The 'general rule' is that 'acquainted persons in a social situation require a reason not to enter' an encounter, 'while unacquainted persons require a reason to do so' (1963a: 124). Some unacquainted persons are more open to overtures from others: they occupy 'exposed' or 'open positions' (police officers, priests, counter staff). Very young or old persons may find themselves in a perpetually exposed position, deemed constantly open to overtures from unacquainted others. They are 'open persons'. Goffman also identifies 'opening persons' like nuns or priests, who are licensed to accost others at will, and 'open regions', where a position of mutual openness is sustained by all the members (a social party, a church congregation).

For the participant the encounter or focused gathering provides:

> ... a single visual and cognitive focus of attention; a mutual and preferential openness to verbal communication; a heightened mutual relevance of acts; an eye-to-eye ecological huddle that maximizes each participant's opportunity to perceive the other participants' monitoring of him ... presence tends to be acknowledged or ratified through expressive signs, and a 'we rationale' is likely to emerge, that is, a sense of the single thing that *we* are doing together at the time. (Goffman 1961b: 18)

In addition there are likely to be little entry and departure ceremonies and signs to acknowledge the initiation and termination of the encounter. Among the participants there will be a 'circular flow of feeling' among the participants and 'corrective compensations for deviant acts'. Goffman always acknowledged that this ideal type would often only be approximated empirically. Not every co-present person may be fully engaged (the 'partly-focused gathering') and where three or more people meet splintering into a 'multifocused gathering' (1963a: 91) is possible.

Focused interaction is made up of 'interchanges' that have a dialogic, statement-reply form. A statement (e.g. a question) attracts a reply (an answer) which may then becomes the basis for a further reply and so forth. A statement or reply is made up of a 'move', defined as 'everything conveyed by an actor during a turn at taking action' (1967: 20). Interchanges therefore minimally consist of two actors each making at least one move. The concept of move underlines Goffman's thoroughly interactional approach to talk (Williams 1980). It is to be distinguished from the notion of 'message', which directs attention to information flow, and the basic unit of conversation analysis (CA), the 'turn at talk', which is the 'slot' in which talk occurs. Goffman uses all three terms. A move is not always equivalent to a turn. When an individual answers, 'It's ten o'clock. Do you have to leave so soon?' two moves occur in a single turn. The associations invoked by the concept of 'move' are also linked to Wittgenstein's notion of language games (cf. 1981a: 24).

Two features distinguish Goffman's general approach to the encounter. One is the centrality of involvement. The other is his refusal to privilege talk among the expressions given and given off in an encounter. Sometimes a nod or a wave can be interactionally equivalent to talk. The concept of 'move' sets talk analytically on a par with the rest of the expressive conduct transpiring at the moment. Robin Williams (1980: 218) writes: 'while turn ... seems to align individuals and their talk, move aligns situations to talk'. The 'natural home' of all expressive conduct is the social situation. Goffman's initial resistance to CA may have stemmed from a perception that conversation was seen as having properties of its own, disconnected from situational proprieties. Clearly, there has been movement on both sides. It is noteworthy that one of CA's co-founders now refers to the field as the study of 'talk-in-interaction'.

A special involvement obligation is found in conversational encounters: the demand on interactants to become spontaneously involved in the talk. Recall that focused gatherings are characterized by a single focus of attention. In the case of conversational encounters, talk provides the cognitive focus and the current talker the official focus of visual attention. 'Joint spontaneous involvement' in a conversation 'is a *unio mystico*, a socialized trance' (1967: 133). When the trance is sustained, interaction is 'euphoric'. Yet departures from this ideal – dysphoric interaction – are all too common. Goffman lists the four standard forms whereby interactants can become alienated from the interaction that ought to absorb them. Instead of being spontaneously caught up in the conversation, the person may exhibit first, external preoccupation, second, self-consciousness, third, interaction-consciousness or finally, other-consciousness. Conjoint spontaneous involvement can be tricky to sustain without lapsing into the embarrassment caused by too little respect for situational proprieties or the boredom created by too strong a sense of tact.

Situational proprieties intricately organize involvement in both unfocused and focused gatherings. As ever, Goffman finds departures from these rules especially instructive (1963a: 216–41). Situational improprieties are less a matter of personality disorder as they are an expression of alienation from the community, social establishments, social relationships and encounters. In sound Durkheimian manner Goffman relentlessly pursues the ways unfocused and focused gatherings are normatively regulated. However, some of his concluding observations strike a different note:

> Even a loosely defined social gathering is still a tight little room; there are more doors leading out of it and more psychologically normal reasons for stepping through them than are dreamt of by those who are always loyal to situational society. (1963a: 241)

Goffman never confuses doing the socially proper thing with the right thing to do.

DRAMATURGY: ENACTING INTERACTION

The 1959 US publication of *The Presentation of Self in Everyday Life*, a book that breathed new life into the ancient 'all the world's a stage' metaphor, inaugurated Goffman's reputation as a sociologist of international stature. The slightly shorter version published by The University of Edinburgh in 1956 had already received outstanding reviews in the main US sociology journals ('one of the most trenchant contributions to social psychology in this generation' and 'a brilliant piece, whose riches have to be directly encountered'). Its Introduction sets out the impression management thesis: individuals constantly 'give' and 'give off' or exude expressions that impress others present. Regardless of the individual's particular motives, this expressive activity projects a given definition of the situation. The impression management thesis is a set of relatively independent social psychological presuppositions (see pp. 35–6 above), not to be confused with 'dramaturgy', the metaphor that drives the book's analytical chapters. The main body of the book analyses the dramaturgical aspects of expressive conduct. Each chapter pursues a dramaturgical concept: performances, teams and teamwork, front and back regions, discrepant roles, communication out of character and the dramaturgical arts of impression management. Goffman rejuvenates the hackneyed 'all the world's a stage' metaphor of role theory. He takes the metaphor forward by concentrating upon the conduct of persons dealing with the exigencies of co-presence. The central concept of performance ('all the activity of a given participant on a given occasion which serves to influence in any way any of the other participants' (1959: 15)) is defined in situational terms. Goffman also gives prominence, as Tom Burns (1992: 112) notes, to two elements of the metaphor that standard role theory overlooks: the audience for the performance and the front stage/back stage distinction. Goffman shows how interactional details can be cogently understood in sociological terms as 'performances' fostered on an 'audience' requiring cooperative 'teamwork' among performers to bring off a desired definition of the situation. Performances may be presented in 'front' regions (such as workplaces or formal ceremonial settings) that are usually differentiated by 'barriers to perception' from 'back regions', the backstage areas (bathrooms, restaurant kitchens, private offices) where performers prepare themselves. Goffman then examines threats to performances stemming from certain roles and certain types of communication conduct. Performances may be threatened by 'discrepant roles' taken by persons who are in a position to learn the secrets of the team (informers, go-betweens and 'non-persons' such as servants). Performances may also be threatened by 'communication out of character', those forms of conduct that challenge the fostered reality such as 'derogation of the absent', 'staging talk' (i.e. talk about the performance's enactment) and teasing. These sources of threat mean that performers need to be skilled at the impression management arts of dramaturgical loyalty, dramaturgical discipline and dramaturgical circumspection. They need also to be prepared to engage in 'protective practices', and 'tact regarding tact'.

Goffman offers a detailed terminology to understand interaction in dramaturgical terms. For example, the central notion of 'performance' is analysed into its constituent parts. One element is the 'front' the individual employs. It includes the physical 'setting' (the degree certificates on the wall of a doctor's surgery) as well as 'personal front', the 'appearance' and 'manner' (the doctor's white coat and confident handling of the patient's injury). Normally some consistency is expected between setting, appearance and manner (1959: 25). Discrepancies quickly arouse concern: the hesitant handling of a surgical implement instantly generates inferences that query professional competence.

Dramaturgy permits a sociological understanding of the vital emotion of embarrassment, a leading manifestation of dysphoric interaction. Embarrassment arises when the assumptions an interactant projects about his/her identity are threatened or discredited by the 'expressive facts' of the situation (1967: 107–8). Embarrassment, Goffman argues, is 'located not in the individual but in the social system wherein he has his several selves' (p. 108). That individuals work to hold embarrassment at bay by preventive and corrective practices shows how central the emotion is to Goffman's sociology and indeed to his view of human nature (Schudson 1984).

Dramaturgy was a metaphor of continuing importance to Goffman. A recurrent theme in his writings was that successful interaction needs not Parsonian role-players fulfilling the institutionalized obligations and expectations of a status but rather dramaturgically skilled interactants sensitive to the immediacy of the social situation. In an important section of *Presentation* entitled 'Reality and contrivance', Goffman is at pains to argue against the notion that dramaturgical action is somehow false, insincere, contrived and dishonest. Individuals do not learn scripts that allow them to know in advance what they will do and what the effect will be. There is just not enough time for that. Rather, individuals are socialized to 'fill in' and 'manage' any part they assume. Everyday conduct derives not from a script but being the kind of person who enacts and sustains the standards of conduct and appearance of their social group. Goffman suggests that 'we all act better than we know' because our conduct in everyday encounters derives not from a script but from 'a command of an idiom, a command that is exercised from moment to moment with little calculation or forethought' (1959: 74).

Goffman uses dramaturgy to highlight the performed or enacted aspect of the presentation of self:

> A status, a position, a social place is not a material thing to be possessed and then displayed; it is a pattern of appropriate conduct, coherent, embellished, and well-articulated. Performed with ease or clumsiness, awareness or not, guile or good faith, it is none the less something that must be enacted and portrayed, something that must be realized. (1959: 75)

Contrived selves as well as the most authentic need to be enacted, performed. Dramaturgy's capacity to cogently bring into the light the unavoidably performative quality of social interaction was precisely why Goffman continually returned to the metaphor. At no point does Goffman suggest that interactants are constantly aware of acting in dramaturgical terms. It is clear that dramaturgy is a conceptual framework for interaction analysis, not a model of the interactant's consciousness (Messinger *et al.* 1962; Edgley 2003). Goffman recognizes that dramaturgical awareness does sometimes arise, for example in his discussion of 'normal appearances' (1971). Appearing normal in public places can involve the interactant in producing 'normalcy shows' for others that convey the absence of threat (1971: 270–1).

Goffman states that he never intended the dramaturgical metaphor to be taken literally. At the beginning and end of *Presentation* he makes it clear that dramaturgy has several 'inadequacies' as a general model of social interaction. These include: (1) theatre offers an openly 'contrived illusion' rather than real events; (2) staged events are rehearsed, real events are not so well-rehearsed; (3) the three parties in theatre (self, other and audience) are collapsed into two in real life (self and other/audience); (4) the risk to the reputation of the stage player is confined to the professional sphere while the interactant potentially risks more in ordinary encounters (at the extreme, of coming to be seen as a 'faulty person'). Admitting that dramaturgy is 'in part a rhetoric and a manoeuvre', Goffman states that 'scaffolds ... are to build other things with and should be erected with an eye to taking them down' (1959: 254). Yet the dramaturgical scaffolding proves too compelling to be left in the yard. It resurfaces in 'Normal appearances' (1971), seems to be finally laid to rest in the 1974 chapter in *Frame Analysis* on theatre, only to reappear eight chapters later as the key to the sociology of story telling. Then, previewing the core themes of his final book, *Forms of Talk*, Goffman states 'I make no large literary claim that social life is but a stage, only a small technical one: that deeply incorporated into the nature of talk are the fundamental requirements of theatricality' (1981a: 4). Dramaturgy proved to be a richly productive metaphor, eventually adaptable to merger with the frame analytic concerns that animated his later work.

GAMES, CALCULATION AND INFORMATION CONTROL

Games long fascinated Goffman, a fascination sometimes held responsible for his apparent portrayal of interaction, and by extension individuals, in excessively rational, opportunist, and manipulative terms. Game models are often linked to the impression management thesis, which depicts the individual managing and controlling information about self. However, it is essential to disentangle the issues. The game metaphor serves several purposes in Goffman's thinking, only one of which is to analyse calculation in interaction. Games first drew Goffman's attention for the fun they are supposed to generate. Later, he came to see games as opportunities for the display of approved attributes of 'character'. It was only in *Strategic Interaction* when Goffman explicitly addressed game theory that the calculative component came to the fore.

The theme of calculation seems to be embedded in Goffman's (1959) initial statement of the impression management thesis. There he makes three interconnected arguments. The first is that individuals possess a general capacity to control their own expressions given and given off, even though the latter may prove harder to comprehensively control than the former. Goffman is simply recognizing that misinformation happens: humans have a general ability to deceive through expressions given and to feign through expressions given off. The second argument commences from Goffman's proposal that regardless of motive, individuals will shape their expressive conduct to influence the definition of the situation and thus to control how others present will respond to them. This second argument seems to lend a calculative motive to the impression management thesis, but interestingly Goffman disconnects calculation from the specific purposes of individuals. Establishing someone's calculative motive can be a tricky matter, easily open to misinterpretation or misunderstanding, so instead he opts for a 'functional or pragmatic view' (1959: 6) that concentrates on the situated consequences of the individual's expressive actions. It considers not motives but how the individual 'effectively' projects a particular definition of the situation, as evident in others' responses to the individual's actions. If there is calculativeness, it arises not from the particular motives ascribed to individuals but rather from Goffman's functional, pragmatic endeavour to locate the meaning of actions in how others respond to them.

The third argument Goffman makes about impression management draws attention to what might be called the witness's or recipient's advantage: the recipient is able to audit both expressions given and given off, whereas the sender of expressive information can only be confident of control over expressions given (1959: 7). In the original formulation of this idea in his dissertation, Goffman argues that recipient's advantage gives rise to the possibility of conversational interaction consisting of 'a constant game of concealment and search' (1953: 84). A crofter's wife finds out whether her guests really liked the meal she serves by observing how quickly the food is raised to the eater's mouth and the zest with which it is chewed. The complication, of course, is that individuals will be aware that they are being so monitored, and thus any attempt the individual makes to redress the asymmetry of recipient's advantage, 'sets the stage for a kind of information game – a potentially infinite cycle of concealment, discovery, false revelation, and rediscovery' (1959: 8). This process, Goffman suggests, works in favour of the initial asymmetry because humans are better at 'piercing an individual's efforts at calculated unintentionality' (1959: 8–9) than they are at manipulating their own actions.

The calculative theme in Goffman emerges out of careful analysis of the individual as expressive interactant. In fact the notion of recipient's advantage turns upside down one commonplace criticism of Goffman: his allegedly calculating, manipulative, 'Machiavellian' view of the individual. Yet here, in the very first few pages of *Presentation*, Goffman claims that individuals tend to be better placed to detect manipulative, strategizing conduct than they are at enacting it. In other words, people are quite good at seeing through calculative conduct. Perhaps what *Presentation*, and also the discussion of information control in *Stigma* demonstrate, is not mischievously calculating conduct at work but simply socially situated intelligence. He shows how people audit and monitor the flow of information about self in interaction to draw the inferences they need to deal with matters at hand.

In three 1960s publications Goffman explores the utility of the game metaphor for his interaction sociology: 'Fun in games' (in *Encounters*), 'Where the action is' (in *Interaction Ritual*) and *Strategic Interaction* (1969). Interestingly, the theme of calculation is not prominent in the first of these publications. In 'Fun in games' Goffman considers what can be learned about encounters in general from games and the fun they are officially expected to produce. Games help Goffman to see that encounters are likewise 'world-building activities' (1961b: 27), creating a realm of meanings that are real to the participants. Like games, encounters are not 'created on the spot', as simple forms of social constructionism imply. Individuals may produce actions in particular situations – a supportive hug, a warm compliment – but they do not invent them (p. 28). Games also help Goffman to shed light on the leading dynamics of encounters:

spontaneous involvement, ease and tension (euphoria and dysphoria) in interaction, incidents and their management, flooding out and those various conversational asides termed 'byplays'.

Goffman concludes by asking, what makes for fun in 'informal social participation' such as parties? Just to suggest that the individual's spontaneous involvement coincides with the involvement deemed obligatory for the encounter begs the question of how that congruence can be achieved. Games provide Goffman with an explanation. An engrossing game is a game that for the participant (1) has a problematic outcome – losses or gains may occur and (2) permits the display of attributes the wider social world values (like 'dexterity, strength, knowledge, intelligence, courage' [p. 68]). He maintains (against Simmel) that during occasions of sociability, social attributes external to the encounter are not held fully in abeyance. Rather they are sifted through a metaphorical membrane that surrounds any encounter. For a party to be successful a balance has to be struck between too much social difference and too little. If the differences between the participants are too great, it will leave them feeling uncomfortable because they will not share enough with the others present. But if the differences are too small, it will just leave them bored with the occasion. The lesson Goffman extracts from games is that 'too much potential loss and gain must be guarded against, as well as too little'(p. 79) if there is to be fun in games, and in euphoria in social encounters more generally.

Fun requires risk, an idea already hinted at in Goffman's epigram in *Presentation*: 'life may not be much of a gamble, but interaction is' (1959: 243). Risk in interaction is addressed directly in 'Where the action is' (1967), an essay based on his work and observations of gambling in Nevada casinos. Two concepts are central to Goffman's analysis, 'action' and 'character', but to get to them we must first discuss a third, 'fatefulness'. Fateful activities and situations are (1) problematic i.e. their outcome has yet to be determined, and (2) consequential i.e. have some influence on the person's later life. Persons engaged in physically dangerous work (e.g. mining) or certain military occupations can expect to encounter fateful situations. However sometimes people will engage in fateful activities for their own sake; they will choose to pursue 'action' in this special sense of the term, and 'gambling is the prototype of action' (1967: 186). Action is evident in activities as diverse as participation in sports, some types of illicit drug taking and pistol duelling.

Action, then, involves the chosen, self-conscious pursuit of fatefulness. To cope with fateful circumstances the person must possess certain 'primary capacities' – the knowledge and skills necessary to accomplish the challenging task. 'Character' is how one handles oneself during the exercise of these capacities, and in particular the extent of one's ability to stand 'correct and steady in the face of sudden pressures' (p. 217). Thus 'weak' character is evidenced by incapacity to behave effectively in fateful circumstances while 'strong' character is indicated when the person is able to 'maintain full self control when the chips are down – whether exerted in regard to moral temptation or task performance' (p. 217). Action and more generally fateful moments provide occasions for the generation, display and testing of character.

Sometimes persons will engage in disputes with others whose consequence is to build up or tear down character. These 'character contests' teach us 'about the mutual implications that can occur when one person's display of character bears upon another's' (p. 239). Character may be tested in various ways: through the giving of affronts, the making of insults, and through the various gestures and comments through which points can be scored. These practices show how 'the logic of fights and duels is an important feature of our daily social life' (p. 258).

Goffman considers action from the standpoints of the individual and the society. Action permits the display of socially-valued qualities of character: courage, integrity, gallantry, composure, presence of mind, dignity and stage confidence are systematically discussed (1967: 218–26). High risk forms of action tend to be highly regulated in modern societies: 'serious action is a serious ride, and rides of this kind are all but arranged out of everyday life' (p. 261). Moreover, persons may well wish to avoid fatefulness because of its inherent dangers: 'in our society, after all, moments are to be lived through, not lived' (p. 260). But too much 'safe and momentless living' is likely to disconnect the individual from opportunities for expressing those values that are associated with character. Commercially-provided action has an important role to play here, being less disruptive than the serious kind.

Action thus provides opportunities for the realization of those positive qualities associated with character. Goffman's analysis is reminiscent of the ironies found in functionalist accounts of deviance. Goffman recognizes that his theory is predicated on a 'romantic division of the world', comprising on the one hand those 'safe and silent places, the home, the well-regulated role in business, industry and the professions' (p. 268), and on the other hand the activities of those (delinquents, criminals, hustlers, sportsmen) who lay part of their selves on the line and who are prepared to jeopardize their character for the sake of a moment. Action provides the occasion for the realization of values that society requires its interactants to possess, even if the opportunities for the expression of these values need to be kept scarce in the interests of preserving those 'safe and silent places'.

Games also play a prominent part in *Strategic Interaction*, a small book containing two papers that Goffman wrote while a visiting fellow at the Center for International Affairs at Harvard in 1966–1967. Thomas Schelling, who had done much to shift game theory from an arcane mathematical specialism to an approach that shed light on real world concerns, worked at the Center at this time. Goffman found useful Schelling's classification of zero-sum games (if you win I lose), coordination games (if you and I each guess the correct solution to a problem we're both winners) and mixed motive games (where you and I must make a choice whether we can reconcile the conflict of a zero-sum game with the cooperative gains of a coordination scenario).

The two papers contained in *Strategic Interaction*, 'Expression games; an analysis of doubts at play' and 'Strategic interaction', respectively analyse deception and calculation in 'mutual dealings', especially of the face-to-face kind. 'Expression games' explores 'one general human capacity' namely, the capacity to 'acquire, reveal and conceal information' (1969a:4). An observer-subject model is employed to examine the assessments that observers make about subjects, who in turn may endeavour to frustrate the observer's assessment. The various possibilities of awareness, mutual awareness and awareness of that mutual awareness are analysed through a typology of moves from the 'unwitting' to the 'counter-uncovering'. The processes Goffman describes have a contest-like character, which is why he terms them 'expression games' (p. 13). When the ceiling is reached Goffman suggests that 'the degeneration of expression' (pp. 58ff.) occurs: the subject's expressions are so overworked for what might be inferred about the subject's intentions that they come to mean nothing. Goffman draws heavily on espionage literature but claims that expression games are endemic to a broad range of social situations: 'surely every adult who has had a friend or a spouse has had occasion to doubt expression of relationship and then to doubt the doubt even while giving the other reasons to suspect that something is being doubted' (p. 81). It is these concerns, Goffman concludes, that make us all a little like espionage agents.

The second essay, 'Strategic interaction' goes beyond issues of assessment of the other's knowledge state to examine the bases of decision making about actions in circumstances that are mutually fateful. In strategic situations every move is fateful because the other parties will try to second guess its basis and implications for subsequent actions. In other words strategic interaction is where each party will make its decision on the basis of what it believes the other parties know including what it knows that the others know about its knowledge and likely strategy.

Goffman maintained that strategic interaction with its concentration on taking the attitude of the other stands close to the concerns of Blumer's symbolic interactionism. Interestingly, he denied any historical link, and went on to propose that strategic interaction offered a closure on questions of mutual awareness that symbolic interactionism lacked. Goffman saw the book as an attempt to establish the potential and limits of game theory. However, the promised utility of the analytical frameworks is not easy to discern, and there is evidence of a consistently low pattern of citation by other social scientists. Nevertheless, Goffman does return to the themes of deceit and the game-like exploitation of mutual knowledge in his subsequent writings, notably the analysis of fabrications in *Frame Analysis* (1974).

The game metaphor in Goffman's writings is not simply a vehicle for developing the strategic manipulation element of his thought. Games also allow Goffman to come to a fuller appreciation of how individuals are caught up in the reality that transpires moment-to-moment in encounters, and how they offer opportunities for the sanctioned display of the valued qualities of 'character'. Goffman weaves together these elements and links them to the ritual metaphor, which is the prime means he uses to explore the moral dimensions of interaction.

INTERACTION RITUAL

In his dissertation Goffman contrasted the tactical and the tactful, maintaining that in addition to taking others into consideration we show consideration for others. This ritual strand has its origins especially in the late, 'symbolist' Durkheim of *The Elementary Forms of the Religious Life* (which Goffman told Jef Verhoeven (1993: 343) he once thought 'a very, very central book'). Ritual for Durkheim was a standardized sequence of talk and activity that directs participants' attention to especially significant objects of thought and feeling. The form of the sequence is more or less invariant and must be enacted – the fundamental rule being no performance, no ritual. Since ritual directs people towards things symbolically significant to them, it involves acts and attitudes of respect. Durkheim contended that rituals build social solidarity among participants and reaffirm shared values. Goffman creatively adapted Durkheim's theory, imaginatively rendering it relevant to the analysis of gatherings:

> In contemporary society ritual performed to stand-in for supernatural entities are everywhere in decay, as are extensive ceremonial agendas involving long strings of obligatory rites. What remains are brief rituals one individual performs for and to another, attesting to civility and goodwill on the performer's part and to the recipient's possession of a small patrimony of sacredness. What remains ... are interpersonal rituals. (1971: 63)

The ritual metaphor denotes a very different set of concerns to game notions. These are summed up in the vocabulary that Goffman typically employs: care, civility, concern, courtesy, goodwill, reassurance, regard, respect, sympathy. Of course, ritual is not simply about expressions of warm regard for the person. It is also a variable property of social interaction, best conceptualized as a continuum with the vocabulary of contempt and insult at the other end. In his earlier writings Goffman concentrates on the main forms (deference and demeanour) and processes (face-work) of interaction rituals. Later work refines some of these ideas but complicates the picture by introducing the ethological notion of 'ritualization'.

In what is just possibly his finest paper, Goffman (1967 [1955]) draws on the Chinese conception of face in order to analyse aspects of the ritual dimension of face-to-face encounters. The person's verbal and non-verbal acts in these encounters are described as the 'line' he takes through which he expresses his view of himself, other participants and the situation. 'Face' is defined as 'the positive social value a person effectively claims for himself by the line others assume he has taken during a particular social contact' (1967: 5). A person's feelings are 'attached' to face but these feelings are sustained in interaction by the person's own acts and those of others. Face is thus an interactional, not a personal construct: the feelings attached to faces are determined by group rules and the current definition of the situation. As Goffman puts it, 'face is something that is diffusely located in the flow of events in the encounter' (p. 7).

The concept of face allows analysis of the lines persons act out in encounters. Sometimes discrediting information crops up, leading the person to be 'in the wrong face'. Sometimes the person is 'out of face' i.e. unready for the encounter. Some lines may involve snubs, digs and bitchiness, all of which threaten someone's face. 'Incidents' like these introduce matters that symbolically threaten someone's face and thus the 'expressive order' of the encounter. Face-work is what is done to counteract incidents and thus sustain the expressive order. Face-work refers to 'actions taken by a person to make whatever he is doing consistent with face' (p. 12). Two basic kinds of face-work are analysed: avoidance practices and corrective practices. Avoidance practices include staying away from times, topics and places where face-threatening acts may occur. The corrective process consists of efforts like apologies to make good the face-threatening act that has occurred. The model of the 'moves' constituting this making good process (challenge, offering, acceptance, thanks) would be much developed later in Goffman's (1971) chapter on 'remedial interchanges'. The intricacies of cooperative and aggressive uses of face-work and the place of face-work in spoken interaction are considered in outline.

Goffman concludes that 'universal human nature is not a very human thing' (1967: 45). It is to be found not in individuals as such but in the need for every society to 'mobilize their members as self-regulating participants in social encounters' (p. 44). The ritual requirements articulated by the face-work model provide one means of so mobilizing individuals.

Goffman develops the ritual theme in 'The nature of deference and demeanor' (1967[1956c]) with the benefit of more ethnographically precise data. He draws upon two months of observational work on two wards in a 'modern research hospital'. Deriving themes from Durkheim's (1915) chapter on the soul in *The Elementary Forms* that Goffman had already identified in his dissertation as of central significance for our understanding of the individual as interactant, Goffman explores 'some of the senses in which the person in our urban secular world is allotted a kind of sacredness that is displayed and confirmed by symbolic acts' (1967: 47). Ritual is explicitly defined by Goffman as 'a way in which the individual must guard and design the symbolic implications of his acts while in the immediate presence of an object that has a special value to him' (p. 57) and two important forms of interpersonal ritual, deference and demeanour, are analysed.

Deference is 'that component of activity which functions as a symbolic means by which appreciation is regularly conveyed *to* a recipient *of* this recipient, or something which this recipient is taken as a symbol, extension or agent' (p. 56). Echoing Durkheim's (1915) distinction between negative and positive rituals, Goffman describes various 'avoidance rituals' (pp. 62ff.) evident, for example, in tactfully keeping off 'sensitive' topics of conversation or showing regard for another's personal space, as well as a range of 'presentational rituals' (p. 71) such as compliments, invitations and the provision of minor services. Demeanour is 'typically conveyed through deportment, dress, and bearing which serves to express to those in his immediate presence that he is a person of certain desirable or undesirable qualities' (p. 77), for example by dressing formally for a job interview. The psychiatric wards Goffman studied provide some occasionally spectacular violations of the customary norms governing deference and demeanour behaviours. Analysis of these departures underscores the significance of deference and demeanour behaviours in society outside the psychiatric ward. In modern society, Goffman concludes, 'many gods have been done away with, but the individual himself stubbornly remains as a deity of considerable importance' (1967: 95). No priestly 'middleman' is needed to interpret these acts, he concludes, because the little gods themselves understand them well enough.

Ritual notions underlie several chapters in *Relations in Public* (1971). They are most directly addressed in 'Supportive interchanges', which investigates the structure of 'access rituals' (chiefly greetings, leave-takings and farewells) and in 'Remedial interchanges', which examines the repair work done in response to an interactional offence. Remedial interchanges involve an offence, an offender and a victim or claimant. Goffman (1971: 108) introduces the notion of a 'virtual offence', the 'worst possible reading' or 'ugliest imaginable significance' that could be attached to act. The point of remedial work is to change that meaning into something more acceptable. This is achieved through the offender's use of accounts, apologies and requests. The cycle of moves between offender and claimant is termed a remedial interchange. The point of the remedial interchange is to restore a proper relationship between offender, victim and the moral rules that bind them both. Goffman carefully dissects the structure of remedial interchanges, deepening the corrective model from 'On face-work' to accommodate the many ways that accounts, apologies, and requests can be done. Goffman's model has proved suggestive for more empirically-oriented inquires of remedial interchange (see, for example, Owen (1983))

In the 1970s Goffman began to incorporate ideas from ethological studies of animal behaviour. Goffman distinguishes the Durkheimian sense of ritual from the ethological version originating from Darwin (usually termed 'ritualization'). The latter refers to how many species communicate through simplified, exaggerated and stylized behaviours that are built into distinctive displays (e.g. displays of aggression or fear). In the case of humans, Goffman suggests, displays are prospective in character, offering not so much communication as evidence of alignment i.e. the position the person 'seems prepared to take up in what is about to happen in the social situation'(1979: 1). Goffman continues to use a Durkheimian notion of ritual (for example, the ritual constraints model to capture the ways talk is designed to show consideration for 'personal feelings'[1981a: 21]) but keeps it distinct from ritualization, which essentially refurbishes the notion of display already present in dramaturgy.

BLURRED GENRES

This last point shows how Goffman was prepared to mix his metaphors when it might lead to a valuable insight. This practice is connected to his attempts to explore the limits of any given metaphor. It gives his writing an analytical density. There are numerous examples of this practice throughout Goffman's work. The dramaturgical and ritual intersect in *The Presentation of Self in Everyday Life* where the moral character of self-presentations is stressed. In presenting ourselves in a certain way, we have a moral right to expect others to treat us in an appropriate fashion.

Ritual and game metaphors are merged in 'On face-work' where persons are depicted as players of a ritual game. In civil inattention and normal appearances the dramaturgical is married to the ritual. Ritual and game metaphors both figure in fateful action; dramaturgy and game are drawn upon to grasp strategic interaction. Goffman was never at the mercy of a metaphor, but rather sought to use metaphors productively, merging elements in the interest of yielding further insight. Goffman was also no respecter of academic territories and conventional boundaries. His capability for exploring the potential of a particular metaphor and his capacity to creatively synthesize elements from different metaphors is why Geertz (1980) identifies Goffman's practice as a 'blurred genre' falling outside conventional conceptions of the social sciences and humanities.

Most of the ideas about the orderliness of interaction discussed in this chapter were developed in the 1950s and 1960s. As can be seen, Goffman's publications orbited around focal concerns but did not result in a single general theory. In this period his project concentrates on the sociology of the interaction order. The result is a series of conceptual frameworks that most generally attempt to connect the properties of individuals to the sociologically relevant characteristics of face-to-face interaction. This pattern continues in his later writings. The next chapter considers Goffman's thinking about frames, which develops aspects of the frameworks already introduced.

4

Framing Experience

PRINCIPLES

Frame Analysis (1974) occupies a unique position in Goffman's writings. Ten years in the making, the book is exceptional as the only place where Goffman explicitly situates his current concerns next to those of theorists such as William James, Alfred Schutz and William I. Thomas. At 576 pages it is quite simply the longest of his 11 books. It is also one of the minority of his books that was written as a monograph rather than as a collection of free standing or interrelated essays. Unlike the titles of Goffman's other books, *Frame Analysis* promises a research method, a technique for analysing 'data', perhaps analogous to content analysis or componential analysis. Was Goffman at last about to supply a coherent method of investigation, a method that was teachable and reproducible? Certainly, in scale, ambition and scope, the book looks like his *magnum opus* and it undoubtedly marked, if not a turning point, then certainly an important new stage in the development of his sociological project. But expectations of methodological rigour raised by the title were not fulfilled, and it received a mixed initial reception from sociologists.

Frame Analysis might be read as Goffman's response to the challenge provided by the rise of ethnomethodology and related phenomenological developments of the late 1960s and early 1970s. Goffman's earlier work had addressed interactional practices from a series of consistently sociological points of view. Frame analysis turned away from these interactional concerns to address an experiential issue: how do individuals make sense of any given 'strip' of activity? A strip is defined as 'any arbitrary slice or cut from the stream of ongoing activity' (1974: 10) – a somewhat broader point of departure than his earlier studies of situated conduct. A strip is 'any raw batch of occurrences' that serves as the place where analysis starts. In principle, any strip can support several interpretations of its sense. For example, what appears to be a dispute between a customer and market stall holder may turn out to be a joke, a misunderstanding, a deception, a rehearsal of a TV script and so on. This aspect of experience had been popularized in sociology by Schutz's (1962; orig. 1945) notion of 'multiple realities'. Any strip of activity, Goffman (1974: 8) noted, can pose a sense-making problem for individuals: 'what is it that is going on here?' Applying the relevant frame to the strip provides the solution.

Thus a frame is a 'schemata of interpretation' that 'allows its user to locate, perceive, identify, and label' (1974: 21) a strip of activity. The frames that give form to our experience are cognitive *and* are grounded in strips. Goffman suggests that frames imply a correspondence or isomorphism between the individual's perception and the organization of the strip so perceived (1974: 26). For example, the insult frame organizes both how an individual *perceives* certain words and gestures and how the words and gestures come to be seen as the *activity* of insulting some person or thing. Through frame analysis Goffman presents a novel interpretation of the ways in which human experience is socially organized.

The core of frame analysis rests on distinctions between three types of frame: the 'primary framework' and two 'transformations' or 'reworkings' of the primary framework: the 'key' and the 'fabrication' (or 'design'). A strip is rendered intelligible by a primary framework. It is primary in that it is the elemental interpretive scheme enabling the individual to make sense of activity that is otherwise meaningless. The use of primary frameworks is such a massive and omnipresent feature of social life that:

> we can hardly glance at anything without applying a primary framework, thereby forming conjectures as to what occurred before and expectations of what is likely to happen now … mere perceiving, then, is a much more active penetration of the world than at first might be thought. (1974: 38)

Primary frameworks may be natural or social: the latter involves 'deeds' or 'guided doings', the former merely 'events'. The totality of a social group's primary frameworks can be called its 'cosmology'. Presumably part of the ethnographer's task is the description of the group's primary frameworks. Strips of activity are made intelligible by primary frameworks, but this intelligibility is not inviolate and particular frames can in principle always be transformed into something else. As Goffman later emphasized:

We face the moment-to-moment possibility (warranted in particular cases or not) that our settled sense of what is going on beyond the current social situation or within it may have to begin to be questioned or changed. (1981b: 68)

Much of Goffman's book is taken up with the general issues arising out of the reworking of frames and the vulnerabilities to which they are subject.

Primary frameworks can be transformed into either keys or fabrications (which might be thought of as secondary frameworks, although Goffman does not use this term). In the case of keyed frames, all the participants are aware that the activity is transformed. In the case of fabrications (or 'designs') there is an asymmetry: the mark has a false belief about the activity, is unaware of the true nature of the transformation that has occurred.

Both keys and fabrications involve the transformation of some portion of an activity that is already intelligible in terms of a primary framework. Thus a strip of activity that is already intelligible as a fight (primary framework) might be keyed if it is reframed as 'playing at fighting' or 'practising a fight' or 'reporting a fight'. A key, therefore, refers to 'the set of conventions by which a given activity, one already meaningful in terms of some primary framework, is transformed into something patterned on this activity but seen by the participants to be something quite else' (1974: 43–4). Importantly, it is definitive of keyed frames that participants are aware that a transformation has occurred. Common keys available 'in our society' include 'make believe' (playful behaviour, day-dreaming, dramatic scriptings), 'contests' (fighting is the principal model for this key), 'ceremonials' (where ordinary conduct is keyed by being invested with special symbolic significance), and 'technical redoings' (practices, demonstrations, experiments, role playing sessions).

Just as a novel can be made into a film and a film can be made into a novel, it is clear that transformations of frames can operate in both directions. Any particular keying is reversible. Crime films may establish a language and style for actual criminals; the detailed reporting of a crime may lead to further crimes modelled after the report. More generally, it seems that keyings are subject to rekeying. For example, plays are usually rehearsed, the rehearsal constituting a rekeying of the keyed frame, the theatrical play. The framing complications created by these possibilities can be controlled if successive transformations are thought of as adding 'layers' or 'laminations' to the activity.

The contrasting reworking of a primary framework is the design or fabrication. These frames are generated when individuals induce others to have a false belief about an activity, for example in con games, hypnosis, secret participant observation and experimental hoaxing. Fabrications are classified along a benign-exploitative axis. Benign fabrication, which includes playful deceit, practical joking and the like, is not carried out against the mark's interest, whereas exploitative fabrications are patently inimical to the mark's private interests.

These three basic frames – primary frameworks, keys and fabrications – can be ordered in two major alignments. The first alignment addresses the presence or absence of a reworking: untransformed activity, framed by primary frameworks, stands on one side, and transformed activity, framed by keys and fabrications, stands on the other. The second alignment concerns the accuracy of the participants' conceptions of frame: in activity framed both by primary frameworks and by keyings – 'straight activity' – the participants' frame conceptions are accurate, whereas in activity framed by fabrications at least one participant will hold an inaccurate frame conception. Goffman proceeds to flesh out this core terminology with analyses of extra-frame activity, the grounding of frames in the real world, frame errors, ambiguities and disputes, and breaks in the applicability of frame.

Goffman states that his frame perspective is 'situational', which amounts to 'a concern for what one individual can be alive to at a particular moment, this often involving a few other particular individuals, and not necessarily restricted to the mutually monitored arena of a face-to-face gathering' (1974: 8). Frame analysis shifts the scope of his work towards the individual's experience and away from the interaction order that up until now had provided the analytic anchor for his studies. His remark that 'the first issue is not interaction but frame' (1974: 127) suggests that frame analysis was intended to undergird his sociology of the interaction order up to this point.

Frame analysis expressly modifies and builds on the well-known ideas of W.I. Thomas and Alfred Schutz. The concept of frame revises voluntaristic construals the Thomas theorem, 'if men define situations as real, they are real in their consequences'. Goffman (1974: 1–2) maintains that participants do not uniquely create definitions of the situation. The frame concept modifies the concept of the definition of the situation in a social direction. The personal negotiation of situations involves discovering or arriving at the socially given frame, not creating it.

The aim of frame analysis broadly coincides with the aims of phenomenological inquiry. Like the social phenomenology of Alfred Schutz, it takes commonsense understanding mediated by the real world activities of persons as the proper focus of analysis. Unlike Schutz, Goffman is not prepared to grant paramount status to the 'world of everyday life', and regards as an oversimplification the notion that the 'natural attitude' is unitary, and does not consider that human experience is best approached from an analysis of the constitutive acts of human consciousness. The acculturated consciousness that is Schutz's starting point is very different from Goffman's social behaviourism that approaches questions about mind, self and consciousness from the objective world of human conduct. Frames are social organizational premises maintained both by consciousness *and* action:

> these frameworks are not merely a matter of mind but correspond in some sense to the way in which an aspect of the activity itself is organized … Organizational premises are involved, and these are something cognition somehow arrives at, not something cognition creates or generates. Given their understanding of what it is that is going on, individuals fit their actions to this understanding and ordinarily find that the ongoing world supports this fitting. These organizational premises – sustained both in the mind and in activity – I call the frame of the activity.
>
> (Goffman 1974: 247)

While phenomenology's questions and topics interest Goffman, its person-centred ('egological') method does not. Frame analysis has thus been aptly described as an American formal or structural phenomenology (Jameson 1976; Frank 1979).

However, the book does not mark a complete rupture with Goffman's own earlier writings. Continuities are evident. The frame concept is first mentioned in the discussion of the 'rules of irrelevance' where Goffman acknowledges Bateson's term and notes that games place a 'frame' around a spate of immediate events, determining the type of 'sense' that will be accorded to everything within the frame (1961b: 20). There is a phenomenological ring to Goffman's suggestion that the 'world-building' character of games allows us to see that ordinary encounters can similarly generate for the participants 'a plane of being, an engine of meaning' (1961b: 26–7). Subsequent pre-*Frame Analysis* works also make casual reference to frames.

Frame Analysis also continues themes first introduced in *Presentation of Self*. Goffman's dramaturgy, in Alvin Gouldner's famously sour commentary, 'declares a moratorium on the conventional distinction between make-believe and reality' (1970: 380). Goffman's first book indicated the existence of a more intimate relation between make-believe and reality than is commonly thought. Now Goffman considers just how the conventional distinction is constituted. The assignment of strips of activity to make-believe or 'reality' is a problematic task precisely because elements of each interpenetrate the other. Goffman questions Schutz's assumption that everyday life is a single distinct, paramount reality in the experience of the individual. An adequate analysis of the everyday, Goffman maintains, would fold in elements of make-believe (day dreaming, joking, theatrical gestures), not divide them off as separate finite provinces of meaning. Goffman spells out this argument at the beginning of the final chapter of *Frame Analysis*:

> So everyday life, real enough in itself, often seems to be a laminated adumbration of a pattern or model that is itself a typification of quite uncertain realm status ... Life may not be an imitation of art, but ordinary conduct, in a sense, is an imitation of the proprieties, a gesture of the exemplary forms, and the primal realization of these ideals belongs more to make-believe than to reality. (1974: 562)

Actual, everyday activity consists of 'quickly changing frames', many of which derive from fanciful, non-literal realms. Hence Goffman's argument:

> that strips of activity, including the figures which people them, must be treated as a single problem for analysis. Realms of being are the proper objects here for study; and here, the everyday is not a special domain to be placed in contrast to the others, but merely another realm. (1974: 564)

There is a more intimate relationship of make-believe to reality than is commonly thought. It is because of the interpenetration of fictive and literal realms that Goffman recommends the close study of each in order to learn about the other.

FRAME ANALYSES

For this reason it is not surprising that Goffman chooses to devote a chapter to the theatrical frame. Goffman acknowledges that 'the language of the theater has become deeply embedded in the sociology from which this study derives' (1974: 124). While Goffman does not provide direct answers to earlier questions about the scope of dramaturgical metaphor, he does discuss two matters bearing on these questions: the concept of performance and the differences between staged and unstaged activity.

A 'restricted' definition of performance is now presented as 'that arrangement which transforms an individual into a stage performer' (p. 124) i.e. someone who can be looked at and scrutinized by an audience without offence being generated. This definition strips 'performance' of its metaphorical connotations. As a more literal conception it permits a distinction between types of performance and enables Goffman to argue that performances vary in terms of their 'purity' i.e. in terms of 'the exclusiveness of the claim of the watchers on the activity they watch' (p. 125). Scripted drama, ballet and orchestral music, provide examples of pure performances (where the principle of 'no audience, no performance' applies) while work performances occurring at construction sites, rehearsals and on-the-spot TV news coverage are given as examples of the impure sort. The circumscribed scope of activities designated as a performance contrasts with the more open usage of the term in *Presentation*.

Goffman undercuts those critics of *Presentation* who queried the general applicability of the dramaturgical model by presenting in frame analytical terms his own version of the significant differences between the stage and real life. He identifies eight 'transcription practices' needed to transform 'a strip of offstage, real activity into a strip of staged being' (1974: 138):

1 A sharp spatial boundary marking off the staged from the unstaged world.
2 The opening up of rooms in order to give audiences access to staged action.
3 A proxemic modification: the spatial alignment of persons 'so that the audience can literally see into the encounter' (p. 140).
4 The focus of attention falls on one person at a time.
5 'Turns at talking tend to be respected to the end' (p. 140).
6 The use of the practice of 'disclosive compensation': audiences are given more information about persons and events on the stage than in everyday life.
7 'Utterances tend to be much longer and more grandiloquent than in ordinary conversation' (p. 143).
8 Everything that occurs on the stage has significance for the development of plot or character.

Actual face-to-face interaction is keyed through these practices in order to be transformed into pure theatrical performance.

Throughout, Goffman engages in an essentially productive critique of Schutz, claiming that the terminology of frame analysis advances inquiry into the general features of human experience popularized by multiple realities theory. As an illustration, consider Goffman's (1974: 145–9) analysis of the radio drama frame. A play or serial broadcast on radio uses a range of conventions to frame its dramatic action. Since transmitted sounds cannot be selectively disattended in the way they readily are in actual social activity, this has to be engineered. A strip of radio framed action might involve one character saying, 'Would you like a splash of soda in your martini?', with the sound effect of soda being squirted into a glass being timed so that it does not overlap the affirmative reply. In radio drama the same practice can mean very different things. In the case of music in radio drama, a phenomenally similar event can have syntactically different functions accorded it. Music can figure in at least three different ways in radio drama: as a staged part of the radio actor's background (staged muzak); as a bridge signalling a change from one scene to another; and as 'a sort of aural version of subtitles', a way of foretelling portentous action. To analyse these features of radio drama in phenomenological terms of the distinctive 'cognitive style' and 'motivational relevancies' attributed to staged action on the radio gives 'an *unnecessarily* vague answer. A specification in terms of frame function says more' (p. 148). For Goffman frame analysis permits a more discriminating dissection of the organization of experience.

Goffman returns to dramaturgical concerns in 'The frame analysis of talk' (1974: 496–559). Much ordinary talk consists of story telling, the crucial constituent of which is a 'replaying', i.e. 'a tale or anecdote ... that recounts a personal experience, not merely reports on an event' (p. 504). The storyteller recreates the information state and understandings as they appeared at the time so as to vicariously place the listener in their position. Goffman shows how replaying is facilitated by the properties of talk – the various forms of embedding, speaker and hearer roles, and so on – leading to the conclusion that there are 'deep-seated similarities' (p. 550) between the theatre's frame structure and that of talk. This argument anticipates a major theme of Goffman's final book, *Forms of Talk*, that 'the fundamental requirements of theatricality' are deeply rooted in the structure of talk.

In the last decade of his life Goffman used frame concepts to deepen his interactional analysis. Frame analysis is especially effective in dealing with an issue his earlier interactional analyses tended to overlook: 'context' (Scheff 2005). Frame supplies the sense in which a strip of interaction is to be taken. So while the main topic of *Gender Advertisements* (1979) is an interaction analysis of gender displays, Goffman devotes its second chapter to the question of how viewers frame pictures. In a sometimes-difficult explication he examines the varying senses in which pictures (and especially advertising photographs) can and cannot be regarded as depictions of some 'real' state of affairs. 'Private' and 'public' pictures are distinguished and 'candid' photographs are differentiated from 'rigged' ones. Goffman draws extensively on the notions of keying and fabrication and concludes that both actual and depicted reality is interpreted in terms of a single viewing and reading competency. Members of society decode lived social reality and various pictorial representations of it in much the same way, picking out the same socially relevant features. Goffman notes how, particularly in public places in urban settings, the individual lives in a 'glimpsed world' (1979: 22). The individual may know little of the biography of strangers encountered on his way, but by paying attention to self-presentational conventions is able to make reasonable inferences about the category of the other, their mood, current undertakings and so forth. These 'glimpsings' provide information which is truncated and abstract but which is quite adequate to the task of dealing with a world of strangers. The same categories that the individual uses to glimpse others and their activities are also used to decode pictures. The sense the reader makes of a picture is parasitic on the reader's wider glimpsing competence.

TALK'S FORMS AND FELICITY'S CONDITION

It is a sign of his catholic approach to interaction analysis that Goffman gives his undivided attention to talk in only his last book, *Forms of Talk* (1981a). Talk for Goffman was always just one of several sociologically relevant aspects of focused interaction. It is conjoint conduct that lodges participants in a shared, intersubjective world. The book's five chapters were written over a period of seven years, the first three being published in academic journals. The predominant theoretical orientation is frame analytic, although as ever there is a different blend of analytic concerns in each chapter. Goffman suggests the book explores the interplay of three broad themes:

1 *The process of ritualization*: 'the moments, looks and vocal sounds we make as an unintended by-product of speaking and listening ... (which) in varying degrees acquire a specialized communicative role in the stream of our behavior, looked to and provided for in connection with the displaying of our alignment to current events' (1981a: 2).
2 *Participation framework*: 'When a word is spoken, all those who happen to be in the perceptual range of the event will have some sort of participation status relative to it' (1981a: 3).
3 *Embedding capacity*: the capacity of our talk to be complexly other- or self-referential, as in the example 'To the best of my recollection I think I said I once lived that sort of life' (1981a: 149).

In his last book we find Goffman using some long-established notions from his interactional systematics along with his more recent interest in ethology linked to the rejuvenation of his sociological perspective by frame analytical concerns. In 'Replies and responses' Goffman seeks to replace the narrow statement-reply format (which he identifies with conversation analysis) with a broader and more open 'reference-response' model. CA's perceived determinism, it is implied, cannot do justice to the flexibility of conversation. Goffman's view is that conversation is a fire that 'can burn anything' and 'the box that conversation stuffs us into is Pandora's' (1981a: 38, 74; but see Schegloff 1988). 'Response cries' makes a case for treating certain terms of 'self-talk' such as 'Oops' or 'Shit!' as responsive to the actor's dramaturgical concerns, displaying to any overhearing audience that a sense of controlled alertness to the immediate environment's vicissitudes has been maintained. As Goffman notes, these seemingly spontaneous outpourings of our animal nature actually are less a flooding out of pre-social nature as a flooding in of social relevance. They save face. 'Footing', the book's central chapter, explicates the various changes in stance to ourselves and co-conversationalists evident in how we produce or receive talk. 'The lecture' illustrates some themes from the previous three papers, especially the lecturer's opportunities for changes in footing. 'Radio Talk' is an extensive study of the remedial work that radio announcers carry out on their own speech. Announcers' self-corrective footings are constrained by the 'frame space' they occupy.

'Footing' is the centrepiece of *Forms of Talk*. It opens with a 1973 newspaper report of President Nixon signing a bill in the Oval Office. Nixon quizzes Helen Thomas, one of a group of journalists assembled to witness the bill-signing ceremony, about attending the event in slacks rather than a dress. In humorous mood the President asks Thomas to do a pirouette to show off her outfit. Thomas is immediately transformed from a participant in a state event to a momentary 'object of approving attention' (1981a: 125). With the onset of the tease, the basis – the footing – on which Ms Thomas entered the Oval Office has been shifted. In 'Footing' Goffman examines these changes of interactional gears and what they imply about how individuals participate in spoken interaction.

The theme has its origin in the role distance concept (1961a), Goffman's attempt to sociologically capture the sparky qualities of interactional life that role theory missed. 'Footing' takes further ideas first introduced in 'The frame analysis of talk' (Goffman 1974). Thus, it is another effort to sociologically grasp the moment-by-moment enactment of identities, with a specific focus on conversational interaction. More formally: 'a change in footing implies a change in the alignment we take up to ourselves and to the others present as expressed in the way we manage the production or reception of an utterance' (1981a: 128).

The nuances of these frame shifts cannot be adequately grasped by conventional sociolinguistic notions of 'speaker' and 'hearer' because these concepts are insensitive to the specifics of the social situation that is talk's 'natural home'. Goffman proposes new concepts, replacing speaker with 'production format' and hearer with (somewhat more confusingly) 'participation framework'. The speaking roles of production format are those of animator, author, and principal. The animator is 'the sounding box' speaking the words. The author is the agent who originates the words, written or spoken. The principal is who believes the words (1981a: 144–5, 226). The footing of the speaker is critically dependent upon the combination of these three roles taken at any moment in talk.

Participation framework is the less satisfactory term that Goffman uses to describe the main axes of hearership. As participants in a conversational encounter, hearers may be ratified or unratified (e.g. overhearers) and addressed or unaddressed (e.g. C standing with A and B who are engaged in a dispute). Participation framework is a confused concept because Goffman sometimes uses 'participation' to include both production and reception roles. It might be better, Levinson (1988) suggests, to replace production format with 'production roles' and participation framework with 'reception roles', and keep 'participation' as the term to cover both. While Goffman makes useful inroads into disaggregating speaker and hearer roles into socially situated elements, Levinson (1988: 172–3) argues he does not go far enough and proposes ten production roles and seven reception roles. Yet even this systematic explication of participant roles does not eliminate the analytical problems, for there remain issues of category assignment. As Levinson (1988: 221) states: 'having a set of participant role categories is one thing – but working out *who* stands in *which when* can be quite another, on a vastly greater plane of complexity'.

The disaggregation of traditional concepts of speaker and hearer in Goffman's hands remains a kind of role analysis, an examination of participant powers. What he did not examine in any detail is how these roles are enacted, how these alignments are interactionally achieved, because they are not assigned unilaterally (Levinson,1988: 176; Zimmerman 1989: 222). For this task it is necessary to consult the records of naturally occurring interaction of the kind collected by conversation analysts.

One good example of such an approach is Steven Clayman's (1992) anlysis of how news interviewers sustain a neutral stance in interaction with their guests. Clayman argues that they must shift their footing so as to achieve a 'formally neutral' posture through techniques such as:

- Prefacing controversial opinion statements to make clear they are not the principal of the remark: 'It is said …'; 'Some people are suggesting …'.
- Re-emphasizing controversial words: 'As the Ambassador said, a collaborator …'.

- Self-repairing their own talk midstream to effect a footing shift: 'But isn't this – critics on the right will say …'.

Footing shifts by interviewers (IRs) most commonly occur when the interviewer cites another's views to get an interview going, or when IR is called upon to present the other side of an argument, or when IR is seeking to generate disagreement among interviewees (IEs), or when criticism is voiced by IE against IR.

Although the concept of footing has made an important theoretical contribution to the social situatedness of ordinary talk, Goffman's formulation requires both more systematic conceptual work to characterize salient production and reception roles, and very different methods from Goffman's own mixture of *ad hoc* observation and intuition for it to be empirically investigated. As with so many of Goffman's leading ideas, to remain true to the spirit of Goffman it becomes necessary to depart from its letter, analytically and methodologically.

In a very general way, Goffman's concepts of framing and footing provide analytic resources to address the important distinction between what is said and what is meant. Frames could be said to provide the appropriate context to make appropriate sense of what is said (Scheff 2005). The concern with the analysis of talk and the question of context is also evident in Goffman's last publication, 'Felicity's condition' (1983b), where he treats context as a matter of what we routinely presuppose and infer in conversation. Here Goffman examines the many allusions and elisions that routinely occur in talk, suggesting that they are possible because of the taken-for-granted background expectations and shared knowledge existing between the speakers as well as their cognizance of prior turns of talk. Singularizing J.L. Austin's (1962) notion of 'felicity conditions', the six key presuppositions necessary for talk to be understandable talk, Goffman boldly identifies a single, yet more basic 'Felicity's condition': 'any arrangement which leads us to judge an individual's verbal acts to be not a manifestation of strangeness' (1983b: 27) or insanity. We are able to display our sanity through how we manage our own words and display that we have understood the words of others. While linguists have pinpointed the surface workings of presuppositions (via concepts of anaphora, deixis, etc.) through which such management and display is done, Goffman proposes that it is necessary to add sociological considerations about the situated character of talk if we want to make any inroads into the analysis of the taken for granted. The relevant sociological concerns are footings, relationships, joint biographies, membership categories ('locaters') as well as turns at talk (1983b: 48). Social considerations must be added to linguistic ones because in the response presence of others:

we find ourselves with one central obligation: to render our behavior understandably relevant to what the other can come to perceive is going on. Whatever else, our activity must be addressed to the other's mind, that is, to the other's capacity to read our words and actions for evidence of our feelings, thoughts and intent. (1983b: 51)

Goffman's last works, then, give detailed attention to the minutiae of conversational interaction, the central topic of his doctoral dissertation, but they do so from the vantage of the expansion of his sociological perspective provided by frame analysis.

5
Asylums

LEARNING FROM THE EXTRAORDINARY

The sociological exploration of the interaction order was always Goffman's primary sociological concern. His most popular writings, however, were his books on mental patients, stigma, and gender. In particular, *Asylums* (1961a) and *Stigma* (1963b) were the books that gave Goffman prominence outside sociology and they remain an enduring source of the humanistic and libertarian understandings of his project. These books, along with the often ill-understood *Gender Advertisements* (1979), concentrate on the situations of persons who are seen as different, disadvantaged, or compromised in some way. There is no easy term to cover this aspect of Goffman's work. Certainly, the term 'deviance' will not do. Although *Asylums* and *Stigma* made a major contribution to labelling theories of deviance, Goffman was uneasy about the free use of the term 'deviance' by sociologists and others. Conceptual precision was lost when different kinds of rule-breaking conduct were lumped together under this all-encompassing concept (1963b: 140–7).

Goffman brings his distinctive interactionist approach to bear on mental illness, stigma and gender, producing analyses that take a quite different form from standard sociological treatments of these topics. They might be considered as applied sociologies of the interaction order. They do not resemble 'case-studies' in the usual sense. Goffman never offered a standard sociological account of the specifics of the populations he chose to study – their demographic and social characteristics.

Instead, he constantly endeavoured to point up the general interactional features and processes they exemplify. As early as his PhD dissertation, Goffman showed a strong appreciation of the power of 'extraordinary events to open our eyes to what ordinarily occurs' (1953: 360). Like Freud, Goffman understood precisely how the odd and unusual could illuminate the routine and taken-for-granted. This assumption provided a methodological rationale for studies of persons whose situated identities placed them in a temporary or more lasting excluded, disadvantaged or subordinate status. Goffman's interest, as ever, lay in deriving general conclusions from interactional manifestations of excluded status. Thus Goffman praises the then-recent tendency of sociologists 'to look into the psychiatric world simply to learn what there could be learned about the general processes of social life' (1957b: 201), instead of playing at 'junior psychiatry' (1961a: xi). The rules mental patients break on hospital wards, he wrote, can lead out towards a general understanding of 'our Anglo-American society' (1967: 48). In *Stigma*, Goffman searches through the traditional fields of social problems, social deviance, criminology and race relations in order to develop a 'coherent analytic perspective' on the situation of the stigmatized. He concludes that these traditional substantive fields may have a 'now purely historic and fortuitous unity' (1963b: 147). His gender studies refuse to recognize that women constitute a distinct analytic category for sociological analysis; instead, his investigations fall under the aegis of 'genderism', a 'sex-class linked behavioural practice' (1977: 305).

TOTAL INSTITUTIONS AND MORAL CAREERS

Asylums, Goffman's study of 'mental patients and other inmates', is probably his best-known book to audiences outside academic sociology. This very widely-quoted work was based on 12 months' ethnographic fieldwork carried out between 1955–1956 at St. Elizabeths Hospital in Washington DC. (The rendering of the hospital's name may look odd to those schooled in British English: 'St.' has a full stop, even though it is a contraction, not an abbreviation of 'Saint', and there is no possessive apostrophe before the 's' in the spelling of 'Elizabeths'. US but not UK editions of *Asylums* correctly follow customary local usage, as I shall.) At the time of Goffman's research, the patient population of St. Elizabeths exceeded 7,000. Goffman's stated aim was to 'learn about the social world of the hospital inmate, as this world is subjectively experienced by him' (1961a: ix). *Asylums* opens with a classic rationale for the method of participation observation:

It was then and still is my belief that any group of persons – prisoners, primitives, pilots, or patients – develop a life of their own that becomes meaningful, reasonable, and normal once you get close to it, and that a good way to learn about any of these worlds is to submit oneself in the company of the members to the daily round of petty contingencies to which they are subject. (1961a: ix–x)

The four essays that make up the book are richly informed by Goffman's research experiences, but *Asylums* is not a conventional ethnography of St. Elizabeths. Goffman makes frequent and detailed reference to his ethnographic observations but in each essay seeks ways of moving beyond the particularities of the hospital he investigated. Philip Manning (1999) captures these generalizing ambitions with his proposal that *Asylums* is not a cultural description and analysis of St. Elizabeths but rather an ethnography of the total institution concept.

The first essay, 'On the characteristics of total institutions' sets the stage for what is to follow. Its theme is that the mental patient can be regarded as one type of 'inmate' and the mental hospital as one type of 'total institution'. Light is shed on the mental patient's situation by comparing it with other types of inmate and total institution. The ethnographic detail of the patient's situation at St. Elizabeths comes to the fore in the middle two essays. A processual perspective is adopted in the second essay 'The moral career of the mental patient' in order to analyse the changing nature of the patient's self on the journey towards, and after admission to, the mental hospital. An analysis of the social bond informs the perspective taken by the third, longest and most ethnographically detailed essay, 'The underlife of a public institution', which shows the myriad ways in which patients attempt to untangle themselves from the hospital's conception of their nature. The closing essay, 'The medical model and mental illness' matches the generality of the opening essay. It presents a critical analysis of the applicability of the medical model for understanding the hospitalization of mental patients. In particular, Goffman addresses the impact of the medical model, considered as a staff ideology, on the redefinition of the patient's self. Thus *Asylums* opens with an organizational analysis and closes with an analysis of its dominant ideology. Sandwiched in between there is a diachronic and a synchronic (processual and snapshot) ethnographic analysis. Read this way, *Asylums* does possess an internal coherence, although as Goffman acknowledges, it is not an integrated text. The merit of writing free-standing essays, Goffman states (1961a: xiii), is that it enables more thorough pursuit of each paper's themes to be achieved.

According to Tom Burns (1992: 142–3), Goffman first heard the term 'total institution' in Everett Hughes' 1952 seminar on institutions at the

University of Chicago. While Goffman does not explicitly acknowledge this source, he states that the idea had been around sociological circles in one guise or another for some time. However, he does acknowledge Howard Rowland's (1939) work on 'segregated communities' and, like Rowland, Goffman underscores resocialization and adjustment processes. The total institution is initially defined by Goffman as a 'place of residence and work where a large number of like-situated individuals, cut off from the wider society for an appreciable period of time, together lead an enclosed, formally administered round of life' (1961a: xiii). Prisons are a prime example but a variety of other types of formal organization (care homes, isolation hospitals, army barracks and convents), each with their own purposes, are included in the category.

Goffman's formal definition of the total institution begins with the observation that in modern societies, the daily round of individuals normally involves a separation of places and times for work, sleep and play. The total institution is a type of social organization that breaks down the barriers that usually separate these three spheres of activity. The four 'common characteristics' of total institutions are identified: (1) the daily round now entirely transpires 'in the same place and under the same authority'; (2) activities are carried out in the company of a batch of like-situated others; (3) activities are timetabled and sequenced by clear rules and a class of officials; (4) all of the scheduled activities are part of a plan designed to realize the goals of the institution (1961a: 6). In addition, the need for the management of people in blocks creates a division between supervisory staff and 'inmates'. There is little social mobility between the two groups and considerable social distance. This is the fundamental social cleavage in the total institution. These organizational features of total institutions provide the backdrop against which Goffman's interactionist analysis can proceed.

Although Goffman does devote space to the 'staff world' and 'institutional ceremonies', 'On the characteristics of total institutions' concentrates on the 'inmate world', especially the various 'mortification processes' to which inmates are subjected. The total institution is the epitome of organizational tyranny and coercion in its efforts to control inmate conduct. It segregates inmates from the wider society, and for this reason the 'batch living' of life in the total institution may properly be contrasted with the 'domestic existence' of family life. Thus a major task that must be undertaken by the organization when a new inmate enters is to suppress those features of the inmate's 'home-world'-based 'presenting culture' that are incompatible with its own conceptions of the inmate. Rather than seeking 'cultural victory' over inmates, total institutions exploit the tension created by differences between home world culture and their own. These differences serve as 'strategic leverage' (Goffman 1961a: 13) in inmate management.

A grim portrait is painted of induction into the organization. Goffman suggests that it is 'civilian selves' that come under attack upon entry to the total institution. The new entrant is subjected to 'a series of abasements, humiliations, and profanations of self' (Goffman 1961a: 14). Inmates are dispossessed of their civilian roles, and sometimes their rights as a citizen. They are 'trimmed' and 'programmed' by 'admission procedures': personal biographies may be recorded, pictures taken, body searches carried out, hair cut, personal belongings removed, and clothing replaced by institutional issue. In these ways inmates are obliged to forego many of their previous sources of self-identification. Inmates may also find themselves subject to unpleasant and painful treatments: they may become unwilling participants in 'obedience tests', 'will-breaking contests' and 'initiation rites'. Physical mutilation or disfigurement may be a possibility. Humiliating deferential acts may have to be performed. In addition, inmates may find that 'territories of the self' are violated. Control over personal information may be lost. Physical and interpersonal contamination may result from enforced association with undesirable others. There are also subtler and more insidious forms of mortification of the inmate's self. The usual relationship that obtains between individuals and their acts may be disrupted by 'looping' (where sullen, sarcastic and derisive remarks become the basis for another assault on self) and 'regimentation' (where everyday activities like washing and dressing are performed to a tight schedule) (pp. 35–41). The ordinary discretion in task accomplishment with its 'personal economy of action' (p. 38) that persons enjoy in their home world is severely curtailed or prohibited. Through the symbolic implications of all these 'direct assaults on the self', inmates are made dramatically aware of the disparity between their former civilian self and the conception now recognized by the organization.

The sum consequence of mortification processes is to deprive the inmate of those resources based in the home world that serve to assure them of their 'adult executive competency' (p. 43). Mortification processes strip the inmate's self of organizationally irrelevant identities and identity resources. But having been thus stripped, the inmate must be 'rebuilt' and given an organizationally appropriate identity. The official means available to the inmate for this task is the privilege system. A proper orientation to its three indispensable elements – house *rules* that prescribe and proscribe inmate conduct; privileges that serve as *rewards* for inmate obedience; and *punishments* meted out for infractions of house rules – produces an acceptable inmate self in the eyes of the staff.

However, there are also other sources for the reconstitution of self that are not officially sanctioned or controlled. One such source is the 'fraternalization process' (Goffman 1961a: 56–8) through which socially distant persons in civil society now find themselves locked in a common fate. 'Mutual support and common counter-moves' tend to develop and inmates receive, as it were, a lesson in the common humanity of their fellows. Another source of reconstitution of self, also frowned on by the staff, is the securing of forbidden satisfactions through various 'secondary adjustments' (pp. 54–5). Thus, the mortified self finds there are a variety of official and unofficial sources available to refashion a new self.

The total institution is so successful in redefining the inmate's self that there tends to be a general absence of high morale and group solidarity among inmates. Resistance tends to be covert and understated. Individual rather than collective lines of adaptation to the privilege system and mortifying processes are the rule. The most typical adaptation is to 'play it cool', but other lines include 'situational withdrawal', 'intransigence', 'colonization' and 'conversion' (see Goffman 1961a: 61–4). Each line represents reconciliation of the tension between the present and home-world based identities of inmates.

The stripping and subsequent reorganization of the inmate's self seldom has a lasting effect after release from the total institution. However, what is significant after leaving is 'proactive status' (p. 72), Goffman's awkward term for the graduate status the institutional experience confers. Sometimes the proactive status is looked on favourably in civilian life, as in the case of those completing officers' training schools; sometimes it is unfavourable, as former mental patients often learn to their cost. Thus, total institutions are potent in redefining the nature of the inmate while inside, but its effects soon fade when the inmate leaves.

In line with Goffman's partisan view, the staff world is given much briefer attention. Total institutional staff are 'people workers' for whom inmates are both objects and products of their occupational activity. Staff are caught in the special moral climate generated by the contradiction between humane standards of treatment on the one hand and organizational demands for efficiency on the other. The rationalizations they develop about the human nature of inmates help them to resolve the contradiction, allowing them to coerce inmates in the name of humane standards and rationality. Similarly, 'institutional ceremonies' (parties and seasonal festivities, open days, religious services) serve to temporarily reduce the social distance between staff and inmates. The unintended consequence of such ceremonies is to lay bare as fiction the otherwise routinely sustained assumption of 'difference in social quality and moral character' (p. 111) of staff and inmates.

In 'The moral career of the mental patient' the mental patient is defined in 'one strictly sociological sense' as someone who has been admitted for treatment to a mental hospital. Entry to mental hospital is socially fateful for whosoever enters as a patient. Excluded from consideration are those who do not 'get caught up in the heavy machinery of mental-hospital servicing' (1961a: 129), such as 'undiscovered candidates' for a mental illness diagnosis and those undergoing private psychotherapy outside a hospital. The patient's 'sick behavior' Goffman boldly contends, 'is not primarily a product of mental illness' but is rather a product of his social distance from his immediate situation (p. 130; but see Manning 1999). The patient's path from his home world to the mental hospital and back to civil society is understood as a 'moral career'. The concept of career is generalized beyond its usual occupational sense to include 'any strand of a person's course through life'. In speaking of a person's *moral* career, Goffman addresses 'the regular sequence of changes that career entails in the person's self and his framework for judging himself and others' (p. 128). This somewhat unusual conception of 'moral' seems closer to the attitudinal notions associated with the word 'morale'. The concept of career, Goffman continues, allows the sociologist to make 'a relatively objective tracing of relatively subjective matters' (p. 168).

Goffman's identification of pre-patient, inpatient and ex-patient phases carries echoes of van Gennep's famous model of the rites of passage (separation, transition, reincorporation). Only pre-patient and inpatient phases are analysed. The 'social beginning' of the patient's career is a record of a 'complainant' taking exception to some item of his face-to-face conduct deemed improper. Patients finds themselves part of an 'alienative coalition'. The complainant, next-of-kin, and 'mediators' (psychiatrists, police, lawyers, social workers) seem, from the point of view of patients, to be collectively conspiring to assure their hospitalization. To the patient these significant others comprise a 'betrayal funnel'. Once hospitalized, the patient may in retrospect feel that, as far as the events leading up to his hospitalization were concerned, 'everyone's current comfort was being busily sustained while his long-range welfare was being undermined' (p. 141). At first the patient may be unwilling to acknowledge the newly acquired patient status, remaining 'out of contact' with other patients. However, mortification processes work to dispose many previous self-conceptions. In time, patients come to terms with the 'privilege system' and the 'ward system'. Although patients may resist the implications of these arrangements through 'self-supporting tales', the balance is always tipped in staff's favour, for they can undercut the tales with discrediting information. Eventually the patient becomes demoralized and, for a time, practises 'the amoral arts of shamelessness' (p. 169).

UNDERLIVES AND TINKERING TRADES

The third, longest and most ethnographically detailed essay in *Asylums* is aptly subtitled 'a study of ways of making out in a mental hospital'. In it Goffman describes an inmate culture rich in 'secondary adjustments' (1961a: 189) that enable mental patients to 'get by' in their day-to-day lives at St. Elizabeths. The essay begins by introducing its key analytical theme the nature of the social bond. Individuals are bonded to social entities by obligations, some of which are 'warm' (attachments), others of which are 'cold' (commitments). To consider someone to be bound by an obligation is to imply something about what sort of person the individual is. But the individual may not meet these obligations to everyone's satisfaction. Goffman writes, 'if every bond implies a broad conception of the person tied by it, we should go on to ask how the individual handles this defining of himself', and it seems that in practice the individual neither completely embraces nor rejects his/her obligations but 'holds himself off from fully embracing all the self-implications of his affiliation, allowing some of his disaffection to be seen even while fulfilling his major obligations' (p. 175). Goffman suggests that 'expressed distance' from obligations is a pervasive feature of social life, a central feature of social being.

Various 'unofficial social arrangements', collectively described as 'secondary adjustments', are how mental patients express distance from the hospital's conception of their self. Secondary adjustments are described as methods of 'getting around the organization's assumptions as to what he should do and get and hence what he should be' (p. 189). Mental patients' 'make-do's', their scavenging, their exploitation of outside contacts, their activities in 'free places', their 'stashes' are all exquisitely described. But Goffman does not romanticize making out practices: mention is made of the prostitution, money-lending, racketeering and blackmail that also figure in the patients' underlife.

Goffman's broader theme, however, is the nature of the social bond. With any social bond there is a conception of the person who fulfils the obligations of that bond. Yet individuals do not simply and always meet these obligations. Goffman's general view is that everyone – including mental patients – has some means of holding off the self-defining implications of a social bond. Secondary adjustments by mental patients are an instance of a more general process whereby the individual employs 'methods to keep some distance, some elbow room, between himself and that with which others assume he should be identified' (p. 319). Secondary adjustments were not 'childish tricks and foolhardy gestures' entirely consistent with patients who are 'ill'. Rather, they 'were carried on by the patient with an air of intelligent down-to-earth determination, sufficient, once the full context was known, to make an outsider feel at home, in a community much more similar to others he has known than different from them' (1961a: 303). Goffman's great accomplishment was his attempt to restore rationality to mental patients, to render their actions intelligible.

The focus of the final essay is the practice and professional ideology of institutional psychiatry. In a paper replete with satire, sarcasm and irony (Fine and Martin 1990), psychiatry is seen as a service occupation (a 'tinkering trade') given the task of fixing malfunctioning persons. But the medical model of mental illness that informs such psychiatric expert servicing is out of step with custodial functions of public mental institutions. This generates a number of contradictions that Goffman condenses thus:

> The limited applicability of the medical model to mental hospitals brings together a doctor who cannot easily afford to construe his activity in other than medical terms and a patient who may well feel he must fight and hate his keepers if any sense is to be made of the hardship he is undergoing. Mental hospitals institutionalize a kind of grotesque of the service relationship. (1961a: 369)

The central difficulty is that the psychiatrist has custodial as well as medical responsibilities and powers, and the former compromises the latter.

ASYLUMS IN PERSPECTIVE

Asylums is Goffman's most cited work in academic and professional literatures. Its wide readership owes something to the way the analysis functions as an ethnographic analogue of Ken Kesey's celebrated novel (and film) *One Flew Over the Cuckoo's Nest*. Unusually, for a book that did not present practical recommendations for change (Goffman ends by admitting that he cannot 'suggest some better way of handling persons called mental patients' (1961a: 384)), it had a major impact on public policy. The ideas presented in *Asylums* influenced the process of deinstitutionalization of the mentally ill, and in the 1960s and 1970s many large mental hospitals in North America and Europe closed down or drastically reduced their inpatient population in favour of non-custodial treatments ('care in the community'). Certainly different countries implemented deinstitutionalization in varying ways and the influence of *Asylums* was neither direct nor necessary in securing change. Nevertheless, Goffman's book is widely acknowledged to have made a major impact in changing the climate of opinion about the consequences of long stays in mental hospitals in the USA and elsewhere (Gronfein 1992; Mechanic 1989).

St. Elizabeths itself has changed dramatically since Goffman's day. Hindsight shows that Goffman studied the hospital at a critical historical juncture. The mid-1950s marked the high water mark in the inpatient population, just before the advent of anti-psychotic drugs revolutionized the treatment of many kinds of mental illness, dramatically reducing the need for prolonged institutional care. According to the First Assistant Physician of St. Elizabeths (who secured Goffman access rights for his fieldwork), in 1955, the year Goffman's fieldwork began, the hospital numbered some 7,500 patients and 2,500 staff (Hoffman 1957: 48). Two decades later the inpatient population had fallen to 2,700. Patient stays were no longer typically measured in years, but in weeks or months, and treatment programmes themselves were much changed (Peele *et al.* 1977). At the beginning of the 1990s the population fell further still to around 1,500. Increasing proportions of patients were coming to be treated on an outpatient basis. The inpatient population in 2005 stood at less than 600. Now property developers eye the handsome grounds of St. Elizabeths with their prime location overlooking the River Potomac and Capitol Hill while federal agencies contemplate the site's potential for housing government offices. After several decades of deinstitutionalization policies, the changed situation of the mental patient has rendered the total institution model if not a historical curiosity, then at least an irrelevance to the substantial numbers of mentally ill persons now 'cared for' in the community. But if Goffman's model has been upstaged by subsequent historical developments, they are developments that Goffman's book helped shape.

Asylums proved to be an appealing but enduringly contentious book. The realism and relevance of Goffman's picture of the mental hospital and its inmates have been questioned. Critical commentary has coalesced around four areas: the organizational analysis; the portrayal of the inmate's experience; fieldwork methods; and the rhetorical force of the writing.

Flaws in Goffman's organizational analysis

Goffman primarily intended the model of the total institution to illuminate aspects of patient life in the mental hospital. Yet his frequent comparison of the mental hospital with prisons and military camps seemed to deny its therapeutic task and emphasize custodial and punitive functions. One reviewer complained that the book was 'muddled by the almost endless provocative descriptive comparisons of mental hospitals with jails, seedy boarding schools, poorly run ships and so on' (Caudill 1962: 368). Such criticisms draw attention to Goffman's lesser ambition of constructing a concept that would permit comparisons between different types of total institution. Thus a body of commentary has concentrated on Goffman's comparative organizational analysis of the total institution and the revisions it seems to require.

It has been frequently noted that Goffman plays up the similarities in practices across different types of total institution while neglecting to examine their differences. In developing a 'general profile' of the total institution Goffman anticipates this criticism and introduces an important caveat. He states that:

> none of the elements I will describe seems peculiar to total institutions, and none seems to be shared by every one of them; what is distinctive about total institutions is that each exhibits to an intense degree many items in this family of attributes. (1961a: 5)

But how well do the four features making up the family of attributes (all aspects of life conducted in one place under a single authority; batch living; tight scheduling of activities guided by official rules; single rational plan fulfilling the institution's aims – see page 71 above) fit with what goes on in different types of total institution? Nick Perry (1974) suggests that a wide range of practices occur under each of Goffman's headings. For example, batch living does not capture well the typical day of a patient in a TB sanatorium or a seafarer in the merchant navy, both of whom spend long periods on their own, not with like-situated others. Perry's suggestion is that for purposes of comparative analysis, Goffman's four features need to be formulated not as characteristics but as variables that would allow the degree of batch living to be identified in an organization. This would be more in keeping with Weber's method of ideal types, which Goffman invokes but misapprehends in his constant highlighting of similarities. If the four features were construed as variables then Goffman's concept could function, as Weber intended the ideal type to work, as a theoretical idealization designed to illuminate how far actual organizations correspond to and depart from the ideal type of total institution.

Other commentators have also argued that Goffman's image of a monolithic organization run along totalitarian lines does not fit the wide range of total institutions found empirically. This image is partly the result of what Christie Davies (1989) calls Goffman's method of 'confirmatory sampling'. Goffman tends to use opportunities for comparison simply to gather further similar examples of patterns he has identified rather than occasions for exploring the range of practices found in different total institutions. By playing down differences Goffman is able to present the total institution as a more homogenous class than is justified. Davies recommends a comparative approach that is sensitive to organizational difference, suggesting three key sources of variation. First, total institutions vary according to the degree of openness or closure of the institution (to what extent is the inmate's entry to the total institution voluntary?). Second, total institutions vary according to their official aim or purpose (is there some external task to perform or is containment or transformation of the inmate the goal?). Third, total institutions vary according to the methods through which inmate compliance to the authority structure is established (by coercion, or by normative appeals or by remuneration?). These distinctions enable key differences between such different kinds of total institutions as brainwashing camps, monasteries and merchant ships to be more clearly identified. Attention to these distinctions also enables an assessment to be made of how 'total' the institution is, how extensive and central is the mortification of the inmate's self, and how likely it is that a cohesive underlife will develop.

A related dispute has been the extent to which it is apt to classify the mental hospital as a total institution. St. Elizabeths, it has been argued, was not typical of mental hospitals as a whole in the mid-1950s. Goffman is said to have over-generalized from one very large public mental hospital at a time when most admissions were involuntary to all mental hospitals, irrespective of their size and admissions profile. This is part of a larger criticism that Goffman's formal or structural approach only succeeds by neglecting the history, policies, staffing and patient profiles of particular hospitals (including the one he intensively studied). On the one hand Goffman can be applauded for his inventiveness and theoretical ambition in devising the concept of the total institution. On the other hand, it is clear that to be of further use in organizational analysis, the concept of the total institution needs further emendation along the lines suggested above in order to address differences between instances of the general class – to systematically explain how and why a Swiss girls' finishing school is a very different total institution to a prisoner of war camp. Characteristically, Goffman took no interest in the subsequent development of his notable contribution to organizational theory.

Relevance of the total institution model to the mental patient's situation

A decontextualizing tendency is also present in Goffman's account of the mental patient's situation, where critics have pointed to important omissions. To appreciate these criticisms the distinctive aspects of Goffman's approach need to be noted. Goffman tells us that he will offer a 'faithful' albeit 'partisan' description of the mental patient's situation, a description that earlier psychiatrically framed accounts neglected. The self and situation of the patient, not the staff, form the analytical focus of *Asylums*. A striking feature of Goffman's approach to the inmate's self is its 'relentlessly sociological character and its relative freedom from imputations of pathology' (Gronfein 1992: 139). In 'Moral career' especially, Goffman conceives the patient self in radically social terms, as a construct dwelling in a pattern of social control generated by the person's place in institutional arrangements. The defining feature of the mental patient is not presence of a mental illness but the way the person's 'social fate' is altered by the fact of hospitalization in a psychiatric institution. Secondary adjustments were not seen as the tricks and games of sick people but rather as rational responses by patients to their situation.

Mental illness is absent as an explanatory factor in Goffman's account of the patient's situation. This characterization of the mental patient as inmate seems to deny that the patient is 'ill' in any substantial sense. Predictably, this claim has drawn criticism, not all of it from the direction of those sympathetic to orthodox psychiatry. Goffman is criticized for failing to differentiate the personal predicaments of individual patients or give the patient's real difficulties the weight they deserve in explaining his or her incarceration (Sedgwick 1982). The strong implication that the therapeutic goals of the hospital are illusory is not supported by the facts, which show some patients benefiting from their hospital treatments. Similarly, the negative and pejorative associations that Goffman attaches to the mortification processes might be regarded as no more than a sociological reading of a wide variety of practices, not all of which will be experienced in this way by inmates. For example, Mouzelis (1971) has used Goffman's own observation that head shaving 'may enrage a mental patient, it may please a monk' to argue that Goffman has forgotten his symbolic interactionism in failing to examine the actual meanings that people attach to mortification processes. But Goffman's point in these pages (1961a: 47–8) *is* an expressly symbolic interactionist one: what matters is how the act can be *read* as a curtailment or mortification of self, and the relevant reference point is the inmate's civilian self. Goffman's interactionist argument involves a sociological appraisal of the implications of institutional arrangements for the inmate self, not a survey of how inmates feel about their current circumstances. Here, as elsewhere, Goffman acknowledges that it is entirely reasonable to expect people's moods and feelings to fluctuate. The mortification of the inmate's self may or may not coincide with the feelings of distress that inmates actually experience, which can change over time. What Goffman is presenting, in other words, is not a phenomenology of the inmate's experience but a sociological rendering of the inmate's point of view drawn from the enactment of institutional arrangements evident in face-to-face conduct. It is not the patient's experience, but rather their situation that Goffman is attempting to portray.

Goffman's field methods

A further source of criticism of *Asylums* has been Goffman's observational method and fieldwork practices at St. Elizabeths. Pretending to be a hospital employee ('assistant to the athletic director') but not carrying the bunch of keys emblematic of staff status, he had maximum freedom to come and go to all parts of the hospital, observing and informally interviewing. He did not sleep in the wards, nor was he directly involved in patients' well-being, which have led some to question how faithfully he represented patients' views. Ethnographic fieldwork research based on the intensive study of one or two sites standardly attracts queries about the representativeness of what the ethnographer has witnessed, for it is often difficult to provide any independent check of the observations made or the inferences drawn. Studies founded on fieldwork often rely on more 'subjective' bases for acceptance, such as the plausibility of the account and the sense of trust the author manages to strike up with the reader. The sketchy details Goffman provides of his fieldwork practices, together with the fragmented, decontextualized manner in which his fieldwork observations are presented, results in an account peopled by faceless mental patients (Fairbrother 1977). In the presentation of his fieldwork observations, Goffman the ethnographer is rarely in evidence.

There is a conspicuous discrepancy between the highly developed reflexivity Goffman ascribes to the human agent and his own fly-on-the-wall 'I am a camera' conception of his fieldwork role. What does this put at risk? Goffman as it were, absents himself from his own acute and astute observations of patient life. By providing a fragmented account that routinely neglects his own lively ethnographic presence, he fails to inspire the confidence that would assure readers that they could share Goffman's interpretations of events (Fairbrother 1977). It is almost as if Goffman's prodigious observational talents render these conventional bases of ethnographic authority redundant. Too often Goffman's writing stuns his readers into agreement with his portrayal.

Twenty years on, in what was admittedly already a changed institution, many of Goffman's observations about secondary adjustments seemed nowhere near as commonplace as Goffman implies (Peele *et al.* 1977). Much later, and after Goffman had lived through his wife's mental illness and suicide, he reported 'that had he been writing *Asylums* at that point, it would have been a very different book' (Mechanic 1989: 148).

Metaphysics and the rhetorical force of *Asylums*

The wide-ranging changes ushered in by deinstitutionalization could be said to leave Goffman's analysis as little more than a historical curiosity (Weinstein 1994). State mental hospitals in the USA, including St. Elizabeths, are much smaller than in Goffman's day and no longer feature a large proportion of involuntary patients. The concept of total institution needs substantial amendment. Yet despite the conceptual, methodological and empirical criticisms, the influence of Goffman's account continues. To understand this, the rhetoric and metaphysics of Goffman's portrayal need to be addressed.

Asylums proved a lightning rod for the growing body of social scientific and philosophical writings critical of the practice of psychiatry and the effects of confinement in a mental hospital. *Asylums* is often bracketed, rightly, with the writings of Foucault, Laing, Szasz and others associated with the 1960s anti-psychiatry movement. According to Andrew Scull (1989: 308–9), *Asylums*

> was simply the most rhetorically persuasive presentation of a widespread scholarly consensus ... The importance of his essays lay ... in the skill with which he deployed then extended conventional wisdom and the adroitness with which he made use of limited evidence of often dubious validity to advance some extremely general claims.

Goffman's concerns are 'metaphysical' as well as sociological: 'the total institution is at once an empirical organization, a symbolic presentation of organizational tyranny, and a closed universe symbolizing the thwarting of human possibilities' (Perry 1974). In this respect *Asylums* echoes the imagery and sentiments of Franz Kafka's novels (especially *The Trial*). These qualities of Goffman's study will ensure that it continues to be read long after many other hospital studies of that era have been forgotten.

THE INSANITY OF PLACE

From the *Asylums* research Goffman derived the view that mental symptoms were best seen as part of the class of behaviours he designated as 'situational improprieties' (1967: 147). One of Goffman's controversial arguments in *Asylums* is that what is seen psychiatrically as a 'mental symptom' can be seen sociologically as a method of expressing distance and disdain for the current circumstances. In Goffman's words:

> If you rob people of all customary means of expressing anger and alienation and put them in a place where they have never had better

reason for these feelings, then the natural recourse will be to seize on what remains – situational improprieties. (1967: 147)

But what of the situation of those with mental symptoms outside the total institution? This question is addressed in his neglected 1969 paper, 'The insanity of place' (1971[1969b]) where Goffman presents his most considerable appraisal of the nature of mental illness. Although not acknowledged, it is likely that it incorporates Goffman's reflections on dealing with his first wife's mental symptoms. His view of the effectiveness of mental hospitals has not shifted ('hopeless storage dumps trimmed in psychiatric paper' (1971: 336)) but he acknowledges much has changed since his mid-1950s work at St. Elizabeths. Instead of speaking of deinstitutionalization, he uses the term 'community containment' to refer to the new circumstances the mentally ill confront.

The key to Goffman's analysis is a distinction between the individual's self and person. 'Person and self are portraits of the same individual', Goffman states 'the first encoded in the actions of others, the second in the actions of the subject himself' (1971: 339). When individuals follow the locally-operating rules, the situational proprieties, there is a consonance between self and person. But if a rule is broken, the actor has not met an obligation and the recipient has a disappointed expectation. So self and person are normatively regulated.

Mental symptoms, Goffman suggests, are seen as a special sub-set of situational improprieties. They are undisguised, repeated and apparently thoroughly wilful, 'specifically and pointedly offensive' (1971: 356). They are carried out by people who refuse to keep their social place as their significant others see it. The mentally ill individual is, through these improprieties, claiming a place and a self that they cannot rightfully claim. In so doing the individual creates 'havoc' for all around (the havoc created in the family is a special concern of Goffman's essay). These situational improprieties are evidence of an incapacity to meet the social obligations normally binding on individuals to keep their place. Thus, Goffman views mental illness not as an attribute of brain malfunctioning by the ill person, nor does he see it (as in some versions of labelling theory) as simply embodied in the reactions of others. Mental illness is founded in troubled relationships between people, within the disruption of the networks and obligations that ordinarily serve to tie them together in a stable and routine manner. The ill person's psychological state may have an organic basis, but it just as easily may not, and it is the diversity of sources of mental symptoms that make the psychiatrist's job so difficult and frequently unsuccessful (1971: 387–9).

6
Spoiled Identity and Gender Difference

STIGMA

While Goffman's ideas on stigma and gender difference belong to different phases of his intellectual production, they each exemplify the 'applied' side of his sociology of the interaction order, exploring the grounds on which persons can find their participation in interaction problematic. These pioneering studies highlight the interactional manifestations of pervasive forms of social disadvantage.

Stigma: Notes on the Management of Spoiled Identity (1963b) has its roots in Goffman's paper on the mental patient's moral career, which identifies an ex-patient phase but does not examine it. At the time he was writing this paper (see Goffman 1957c), it is clear that he wanted to link the ex-patient's difficulties to other categories of person who faced comparable troubles: the disfigured and physically handicapped, the deaf and the blind, the ex-convict, the alcoholic, the addict, the member of an ethnic minority and so on. All these persons frequently find themselves in situations where they are stigmatized i.e. 'disqualified from full social acceptance' (1963b: Preface). Although a stigma is defined by Goffman as a 'deeply discrediting attribute', he insists that the sociological study of stigma demands 'a language of relationships, not attributes' (p. 3), since what will count as a stigma is responsive to the particularities of local contexts. The worries of a professional criminal about being seen entering a library is one example Goffman gives of just how varied stigmatizing attributes can be.

The core of *Stigma*'s impressive conceptual architecture lies in the three notions of identity Goffman deploys. In successive chapters Goffman introduces the concepts of 'social identity', 'personal identity' and 'ego or felt identity'. Broadly, Goffman intends *social identity* to refer to the everyday ways persons are identified and categorized, *personal identity* to what marks out the person as distinct from all others, and *ego or felt identity* to refer to the feelings that a person has about their identity. Goffman identifies a set of social processes characteristically associated with each of these identity concepts. *Stigma* is also notable for its extensive use of first-person accounts drawn from popular biographies and autobiographies, social histories, and case materials from social science sources. Substantial quotations from these sources not only illustrate Goffman's sociological analysis; they also vividly and concretely depict the plight of the stigmatized and encourage identification and sympathy towards their predicaments.

Goffman begins with the concept of social identity, the category and attributes of a person that are available to us on first appearance. Social identity is a better term than social status to describe these attributes because it invokes personal qualities like 'honesty' in addition to the structural features, such as 'occupation', that social status includes. Goffman further develops this identity concept with a distinction between 'virtual' and 'actual social identity'. Virtual social identity concerns the assumptions and anticipations that we make 'in effect' about people on the basis of first appearances. Actual social identity is the category and attributes that experience proves a person to possess (p. 2). Interaction proceeds smoothly when virtual and actual identities match. When they are discrepant or incongruent, then there is potential for disruption. But not just any discrepancy will produce the 'shameful differentness' characteristic of stigma. It is only when the discrepancy works to discredit and downgrade our initial anticipations, rather than to elevate them, that we can properly speak of stigma. While the notion of a virtual/actual discrepancy is echoed elsewhere in Goffman's writings (for example, on embarrassment and on remedial interchanges), it is difficult to disagree with Burns' (1992: 217) assessment that here the distinction complicates more than it illuminates. Perhaps more helpful in describing the scope of stigma are the three broad types Goffman proceeds to introduce: (1) physical deformities, (2) character faults and blemishes (dishonesty, addiction, weak will) and (3) 'the tribal stigma of race, nation and religion' (p. 4).

The next conceptual pairing Goffman introduces is more central to his task. Plainly, some kinds of stigmatic attributes can be concealed. This possibility gives rise to two classes of possessor: the 'discredited', the stigmatized who can assume that their stigma is evident in any encounter with 'normals', and the 'discreditable', whose stigma is not observable or otherwise available (p. 4). Goffman treats the social identity of the discredited as his main concern in the first chapter, reserving consideration of the discreditable to the next. Focusing on the social identity of the discredited enables Goffman to examine the broad processes of stigmatization. Goffman notes the 'pivotal fact' (p. 7) that overwhelmingly the discredited tend to hold the same identity beliefs as normals. In a memorable flourish, he declares that the 'mixed contacts' between normals and stigmatized present 'one of the primal scenes of sociology'(pp. 12–13).

A basic interactional problem is the management of tension between normals and stigmatized. Two categories of 'sympathetic other' (p. 19), people who share the characteristic feelings and standpoints of the stigmatized, help in the management of this tension: the 'own' and the 'wise'. While the own actually possess the same stigma as the discredited person, the wise are those persons (such as family members) who are knowledgeable about the discredited person's predicament. Through their direct acquaintance with the discredited person they may acquire a 'courtesy stigma' (p. 30). Goffman discusses the different 'moral careers' the stigmatized may experience. These are the typical patterns of learning and changes in conceptions of self that personal adjustment to the stigma requires. Those who are born with a stigma face different moral careers than those who acquire one later in life.

Goffman's attention then turns to the discreditable. As their stigma is not immediately apparent, controlling the flow of information about it is the discreditable's basic interactional problem. Information control for the discreditable is a thoroughly contextual matter: 'To display or not to display; to tell or not to tell; to let on or not to let on; to lie or not to lie; and in each case, to whom, how, and where' (p. 42). At the heart of this process is the notion of personal identity, the sense of uniqueness we develop about an individual through knowledge of the distinctive 'identity pegs', 'positive marks' and life history information (held in memory or file) we associate with them (p. 56). To disclose information about a stigma is to disclose a potentially damaging aspect of one's personal identity. There will be many circumstances, therefore, where the discreditable will guard their personal identity by strategic management of information about self. In a chapter occupying nearly half the book, Goffman explores the interactional strategies and contingencies that operate as discreditable persons seek to control information about their stigma. Much is made of the 'reflexive' and 'embodied' character of information about stigma: 'it is conveyed by the very person it is about, and conveyed through bodily expression in the immediate presence of those who receive the expression' (p. 43). The largest part of the chapter is devoted to a critical application of the arts of impression management to the discreditable's situation. The centrality of 'visibility' or 'evidentness' (p. 48) of a stigma is stressed. The general properties of 'biography' and 'biographical others' in the management of stigma are examined in a discussion that runs directly counter to the common view that Goffman lacks a conception of the continuity of the person and the importance of memory (p. 65). The lengthy discussion of 'passing' (pp. 73–91) considers the vicissitudes attendant upon attempting to conceal a stigma in everyday life. The difficulties faced by the prostitute in hiding her occupation from relatives, the alcoholic in concealing his inebriation at work or the married homosexual explaining his unusual choice of beneficiary for the house insurance are detailed. Linked to passing is another set of techniques where the aim is not concealment but minimization of the obtrusiveness of the stigma during mixed contacts with normals. Such practices of 'covering' include those blind people who wear dark glasses to conceal the facial disfigurement associated with their condition – a case of 'revealing unsightedness while concealing unsightliness' (p. 103).

'Ego' or 'felt identity' is 'the subjective sense of his own situation and own continuity and character that an individual comes to obtain as a result of his various social experiences' (p. 105). This concept facilitates analysis of what the individual feels about his stigma, its management, and the various sources of advice provided to the stigmatized individual. Some 'ambivalence' towards other, like-situated persons is commonly experienced by the stigmatized, as is the tendency towards the development of 'professional presentations' to handle such ambivalence. Additionally, the individual may be torn between contrasting loyalties to and identifications with those sharing the stigma and normals. The pulls of these 'in-group' and 'out-group alignments' may produce a conflict of possible ego identities. The often-touted 'good adjustment' of the stigmatized to their condition, Goffman argues, frequently masks the 'phantom acceptance' and 'phantom normalcy' (p. 122) they may actually experience. There is no easy good adjustment but merely the play of contrasting identifications likely to lead to a 'politics of identity' where the stigmatized are caught in the cross-fire of arguments about what their ego identity ought really to be (pp. 123–5).

One of Goffman's achievements is to develop a firm sense that difference is not deviance, or at least not deviance in any consequential meaning of the term. As noted, Goffman complains that sociologists have been too quick to take up the term 'deviance' and use it to label all manner of human conduct. If the stigmatized person is a deviant then s/he is a 'normal deviant' Goffman (1963b: 131) suggests, the normal prefix being used to indicate how commonplace the status is. On the other hand Goffman (1963b: 143–4) reserves the term 'social deviant' for a range of persons ('prostitutes, drug addicts, delinquents, criminals …') who are 'engaged in some kind of collective denial of the social order', representing what is often regarded as culturally or politically inspired resistance to society's 'approved runways' and its 'motivational schemes'.

Goffman's argument shows how stigma dynamics are not the sole preserve of particular categories of person such as the physically handicapped or ethnic minorities but rather are part of a very general social process, experienced by everyone at some point in their lives. Every society has very widely held norms about identity or being that serve as a basis for 'grading' (Burns 1992) persons. Some identity norms are sustained routinely and on a widespread basis, such as sightedness and literacy while others, such as physical beauty, present ideals that few people can ever fully realize:

> … in an important sense there is only one complete unblushing male in America: a young, married, white, urban, northern, heterosexual Protestant father of college education, fully employed, of good complexion, weight and height, and a recent record in sports.
>
> (Goffman 1963b: 128)

Deviations from identity norms are therefore very common. Goffman maintains it would be pointless to count the number of stigmatized because everyone, 'if for no other reason than oncoming agedness' (p. 129), will have personal experience of a variety of stigmas. Stigma management is thus a very general social process pertaining to 'shameful differences' (p. 131), not one restricted to an outcast class. It follows that there are no psychological differences between normals and stigmatized since both are cut 'from the same standard cloth.' 'A stigmatized person' says Goffman (1963b: 134), 'is first of all like anyone else, trained first of all in others' views of persons like himself.' He suggests there is a 'self-other, normal-stigmatized unity' (p. 132), not two piles of persons because normal and stigmatized 'are not persons but rather perspectives' (p. 138), creatures of the interaction roles they play, not the attributes they display. When seen in these enacted, interactional terms, the human nature of the other as stigmatized is no worse or better than the human nature of the normal. Stigma concerns matters of difference, Goffman insists, not deviance.

In discussing normal and stigmatized, Goffman's emphasis throughout is that they are interactional roles. Certain persons may play the stigmatized role more frequently than others, but all of us at some time or other find ourselves in that situation. Goffman writes: 'the issue is not whether a person has experience with a stigma of his own, because he has, but rather how many varieties he has had his own experience with' (p. 129). Although interactionally consequential, the categories of normal and stigmatized are not grounded in types of person, which is the widespread belief often used to justify the discrimination the stigmatized commonly face. In *Stigma*, Goffman pursues one leading theme of his sociology, control of information about self, to demonstrate the capacity of his interactional analysis to illuminate the intricacies of human difference. The denial of other persons' humanity implicit in acts of stigmatization (Nussbaum 2004) is never far from the surface of Goffman's arguments. At the back of Goffman's dispassionate analysis is a finely honed sympathy towards persons facing a wide range of personal predicaments. While Goffman was a strong writer working from his own distinctive vantage point, he avoids a stance superior to his subjects. *Stigma*, then, is perhaps his most morally compelling work.

GENDER DIFFERENCE

Goffman further explores the complexities of human difference in a book and a paper on gender. The album-sized book, *Gender Advertisements* (1979) was originally published in 1976 as a special issue of *Studies in the Anthropology of Visual Communication*; the 1977 paper, 'The arrangement between the sexes' was published in a theory journal edited by Alvin Gouldner. From the late 1960s onwards feminism placed the situation, and especially the disadvantages, faced by women on political and academic agendas. Goffman obliquely acknowledges the influence of feminism on his thinking at the beginning of the paper that provides his most general statement on gender. 'As usual in recent years', he writes, 'we have had to rely on the discontented to remind us of our subject matter' (1977: 301). But his awareness of the social significance of gender goes back much further. One early example, from his 1953 dissertation, is his remark that a 'woman who is an ardent feminist may be offended if her sexual status is not allowed to remain irrelevant as a determinant of treatment in certain kinds of situations' (1953a: 100). George Gonos (1980: 168n. 52) writes of a 'low burning feminism' found throughout Goffman's writings. What this feminism (if such it be) amounts to is a persistent and acute awareness of how women's gender can be interactionally consequential. Goffman's attentiveness to the limitation that his own gender may have placed on his observational work also predates the rise of current feminist-inspired concerns. His disclaimer in the 'Preface' to *Asylums*: 'I want to warn that my view is probably too much that of a middle-class male' (1961a: x), was certainly unusual for 1961, predating by more than a decade the sensitivity that sociological ethnographers developed toward the significance of gender in field research. In other respects it seems that Goffman was not as gender aware in his 1960s work as he later became. Gardner's (1989) observational and interview findings suggest that Goffman did not appreciate just how thoroughly gendered are people's experiences of public places.

When Goffman's analytical focus fell squarely on gender relations in 'The arrangement between the sexes', his approach characteristically enough was to consider interactional practices. But less characteristically, Goffman is not so much interested in the practices themselves and what they imply for self and social situations as he is concerned with the consequences of gendered practices for the production of gender as a social institution. Goffman's analysis of the sources of gender difference carries a strong anti-essentialism, one that is rather more congenial to feminist concerns than is sometimes appreciated, for he emphasizes its thoroughly socially-constructed nature. Goffman begins by dismissing traditional biological justifications for women's subordination. At least in modern societies, he maintains, far too much is made socially of women's capacities surrounding the temporary constraints of childbearing:

> Women do and men don't gestate, breast-feed infants, and menstruate as part of their biological character. So, too, women on the whole are smaller and lighter boned and muscled than men. For these physical facts of life to have no appreciable social consequence would take a little organizing, but, at least by modern standards, not much. (1977: 301)

Yet societies elaborate and extend these 'physical facts of life' into a major source of essential social differences between men and women. It is this process of seizing upon gender as a marker of abiding social difference between persons that is at the heart of the 'institutional reflexivity' theory set out in his often-overlooked 1977 essay.

The differential treatment of males and females is commonly justified by folk beliefs about presumed 'essential' (biological, temperamental, etc.) differences between the sexes. Goffman turns such commonsense reasoning on its head. Biological differences, he says, rationalize but do not account for this differential treatment of men and women, girls and boys. Goffman proposes that many institutionalized social practices, frequently presented and excused as natural *consequences* of the differences between the sexes, are actually the means through which those self-same differences are honoured and *produced*. For Goffman biology is not an 'external constraint upon ... social organization' (p. 313). Institutional reflexivity is Goffman's term to describe how social environments are constructed to highlight and magnify gender differences. Differential treatment along gender lines results from this process, which is then justified or excused in terms of notions of innate biological differences between males and females.

Goffman gives five examples of the process of institutional reflexivity at work. First, a gendered division of labour encourages couple formation by creating a mutual dependency between husband and wife, so that each has reason to seek the other out. Certain kinds of domestic work are defined as inappropriate for men and certain kinds of paid work unusual for women. Acquiring a spouse therefore offers rewards, albeit different ones, to both partners. Second, 'siblings as socializers' refers to the reciprocal socialization that occurs in households. Gender is appealed to as a basis for giving the girl a softer bed and the boy a bigger portion of food. Brothers learn from their sisters about their own gender identity, and vice-versa: 'It is as if society had planted a brother with sisters so that women could from the beginning learn their place, and a sister with brothers so that men could learn their place' (1977: 314). Third, the gendered division of toilet arrangements in public places segregates the sexes, but as toilet facilities in private households imply, there is nothing in the biology of elimination that requires such a division. Fourth, a system of 'selective job placement' ensures that women predominate in 'meet the public' roles where their appearance is important, thus lending a sexual tinge to many of the dealings men have outside the home. Finally, an 'identification system' marks out persons in gendered terms by sight, tone of voice, first name and title that bias categorization of persons in sex-class terms.

In each of these examples of institutional reflexivity Goffman is at pains to show that appeals to biology and neighbouring forms of essentialism disguise the phenomenon they actually produce: gender difference. 'Gender', he states, 'not religion is the opiate of the masses' (1977: 315). Gender difference is produced and reproduced through institutionalized social practices and beliefs such as the five considered above and the ordinary interaction they sustain. Further, these practices and beliefs hold definite implications for the presumed human nature of gendered persons. Far from reflecting supposedly biologically-based differences in our human natures, institutionalized practices and beliefs are the real source of the differences between the presumed natures of the sexes, their gender identity. When these practices and beliefs are projected on to interactional fields, the resulting scenes 'do not so much allow for the expression of natural differences between the sexes as for the production of that difference itself' (1977: 324).

In *Gender Advertisements* Goffman's attention shifts from the institutionalized practice and belief productive of gender identity to the interactional manifestations of its display. But the book's cataloguing of gender displays is an extension and application of the 'institutional reflexivity' theory of gender differentiation set out earlier. Gender displays are the taken for granted ways of conducting ourselves that bespeak of our femininity ('tilting one's head' in a characteristically feminine manner) or our masculinity ('grasping an object' in characteristically masculine manner).

The critique of common sense biological thinking about gender is taken further in *Gender Advertisements*. Gender displays are most emphatically not to be regarded as residues or remnants of the evolutionary development of the human species, nor are they 'natural expressions' of our supposedly 'essential' nature as men and women. Instead, Goffman contends that 'there is only a schedule for the portrayal of gender ... only evidence of the practice between the sexes of choreographing behaviourally a portrait of relationship' (1979: 8). Persons as gendered agents enact an appropriate schedule of gender displays. Nor are the displays to be treated simply as part of the froth of social existence. In the hierarchical relations between the sexes they are 'the shadow *and* the substance' (p. 6) of gendered social life. Gender displays serve to affirm basic social arrangements (keeping women in their place) and they present ultimate conceptions of the nature of persons (our 'essential' gender identity). These displays are suffused with a behavioural vocabulary redolent of parent–child relationships. The 'orientation license', 'protective intercession', 'benign control', 'indulgence priorities', 'erasability of offense' and 'non-person treatment' that parents ideally extend to children also serve as a model that characterizes the socially situated treatment of adult women by men. Thus, 'ritually speaking, females are equivalent to subordinate males and both are equivalent to children' (1979: 5).

Most of the book is devoted to a novel 'pictorial pattern analysis' (1979: 25) of the presentation of gender (and femininity in particular) in advertisements and other public pictures. Goffman analyses six aspects of gender display evident in his collection of advertising images: first, 'relative size': men are depicted as physically bigger than women, the physical size difference connoting a difference in 'social weight'; second, 'the feminine touch': women delicately touch objects while men firmly grasp them, a pattern that symbolizes their presumed natures; third, 'function ranking': if an executive role can be taken in the situation, the male figure will assume it; fourth, 'the family': relationships between family members can be readily symbolized by spatial positioning within a photograph; fifth, 'the ritualization of subordination': the various gestures of lowering of the body relative to another's that symbolize subordinate status;

sixth, 'licensed withdrawal': the expressions that effect psychological removal from the immediate situation.

A unique feature of *Gender Advertisements* is the layout of the long pictorial section. Arrays of numbered pictures are accompanied by an understated interpretive commentary that gives each page a highly distinctive look. Goffman's procedure is first to present us with his written observations about a particular gender display. These observations are then followed by a series of advertising images that 'illustrate' the themes earlier articulated in words. The pictures are 'arranged to be "read" from top to bottom, column to column, across the page' (1979: 26). Sometimes the series is concluded with exceptions ('sex role reversals') that presumably prove the rule, or at least its typicality. These exceptions are identified by black edging surrounding the picture.

The reader thus has to engage in search procedure, scanning each series of pictures for evidence of the gender display Goffman has just described in words. The reader inspects the series of pictures looking for a family resemblance in the collection and, to the extent that the reader finds the resemblance Goffman has indicated, the written description is corroborated visually. Such co-option of the reader into the process of analysis is a general feature of Goffman's writings (see Chapter 8 below). However Goffman's pictorial data and their relationship to the written text make it a particularly conspicuous feature of this volume.

Goffman's presentation of arrays of carefully chosen advertising photographs has the considerable advantage of allowing subtle features of gender displays to be *exhibited,* not merely described. The persuasive force of this analytical strategy depends partly upon how the pictures are made to function as illustrations of an analytic theme. The pictures appear to have a broadly equivalent function to transcripts in conversation analysis. Like transcripts they seem to allow readers the opportunity to assess the adequacy of the interpretations presented by Goffman, to see how far his reading of the pictures works for us. Readers are required to undertake considerable interpretive work on these pages. The reader must engage in a kind of instructed viewing (to adapt Watson's (1999) notion of 'instructed reading'), a process in which Goffman's written text directs the reader to find, for example, 'body clowning' in the array of pictures presented (Goffman 1979: 52–3).

In these writings Goffman provides a general theory of gender difference and a highly original application of the theory to contemporary advertising imagery. While the picture book has been widely applauded for its innovative integration of written and pictorial text, the institutional reflexivity theory of gender difference underpinning it has been overlooked.

The initial feminist reception was less than enthusiastic, concentrating more on Goffman's imagery rather than his analysis. Janet Wedel (1978: 113) suggested that Goffman 'restates early post-Victorian stereotypes of male–female interaction in all their logical contradictions'. The historical record of women's disadvantage has provided the intellectual and moral impetus for feminist analyses. Goffman's writing on gender derives from a different vantage: 'the sociologically interesting thing about a disadvantaged category is not the painfulness of the disadvantage, but the bearing of the social structure on its generation and stability' (1977: 307). More recent appraisals recognize the importance of Goffman's sociological approach to feminist concerns. Candace West (1996) shows how the institutional reflexivity theory has been amended and developed in empirical studies of gendered socialization and conversational practices. The persistent social constructionism of Goffman's analysis seems to anticipate certain core themes and accents in Judith Butler's (1990) celebrated performative conception of gender. The constructionism informing Goffman's (1977: 305) comment that 'one should think of sex as a property of organisms, not as a class of them' is attuned to Butler's claim that both sex and gender are cultural, not that the latter overlays the former. Compare the following two passages, noting the repetition of the phrase 'there is no gender identity':

> Gender is a 'doing', ... though not a doing by a subject who might be said to preexist the deed ... there is no being behind the doing ... the deed is everything ... there is no gender identity behind the expressions of identity ... identity is performatively constituted by the very 'expressions' that are said to be its results.
>
> (Butler 1990: 25)

> What the human nature of males and females really consists of ... is a capacity to learn to provide and to read depictions of masculinity and femininity and a willingness to adhere to a schedule for presenting these pictures, and this capacity they have by virtue of being persons, not females or males. One might just as well say there is no gender identity. There is only a schedule for the portrayal of gender ... There is only evidence of the practice between the sexes of choreographing behaviorally a portrait of relationship.
>
> (Goffman 1979: 8)

Some of the themes that Butler was to popularize in the 1990s are prefigured by more than a decade in Goffman's gender writings. Goffman offers a sociological basis for investigating the 'personal' aspects of life that feminism has long held to be intrinsically 'political'.

7
Self

TERMS FOR THE HUMAN BEING

When seen up close, the individual, bringing together in various ways all the connections that he has in life, becomes a blur. (1961b: 143)

As an 'ethnographer of small entities' (Verhoeven 1993: 323) Goffman found that his sociology could not help but discuss individual selves. Goffman's thinking about the individual was every bit as controversial as was his conception of sociological method (discussed in the next chapter). Critics frequently disapproved of what they saw as his elevation of the predatory, inauthentic and manipulative dimensions of human nature. His sociology is notorious for use of terms like ploys, stratagems, plots, devices, concealments and the like. Humanistic critics fault Goffman for his apparent promotion of a dark image of humans as cynical opportunists ruthlessly pursuing their amoral interests by managing impressions and controlling information. Before the merits of such judgements can be assessed, we need first to consider how accurate is this characterization of Goffman's conception of the self.

An immediate difficulty is that Goffman is not consistent in his use of such key terms for the human being as self, the individual and person (Manning 1976; Cahill 1998). This complicates the task of tracing continuities and developments in Goffman's thinking. Often, Goffman simply follows standard usage in regarding 'self' as the seat of conscious awareness and identity, 'individual' as carrying notions of singularity and distinctness, and 'person' as implying an embodied agent who acts in some capacity. Goffman also draws upon established Chicagoan notions, particularly to emphasize the social character of personhood. He quotes Robert E. Park's 1926 formulation: 'We come into the world as individuals, achieve character, and become persons' (1959: 20). Goffman seems to endorse Park's conception of the person as a role player with mask in place ('our truer self' Park says, 'the self we would like to be'). Goffman broadly employs the terms individual, self and person in these ways, although his usage is not consistent across his writings. As we shall see, the term 'self' is especially troublesome in this regard. Goffman conceptualizes self in a range of ways across his writings as his thinking develops. For example, the self of 'Moral career' is said to reside in prevailing social system arrangements (1961a: 168), which contrasts with 'The insanity of place' self as a 'portrait' of the individual encoded 'in the actions of the subject himself' (1971: 341). A significant change is announced in 1971 when Goffman suggests the need to introduce a range of 'technically-defined terms' because the notions 'individual' and 'person' prove too imprecise for 'fine-grain analysis' (1971: 3–5, 27). Even so, self does not completely disappear from the later writings – the concept is just too flexible to be so readily abandoned – but it is augmented by terms such as 'participation status' and its frame analytic offspring.

This chapter presents an ordering of Goffman's thinking about self, an ordering that is absent in Goffman's own writings. In common with other attempts at charting the individual in Goffman's writings (e.g. Czyzewski 1987), what follows is a reconstruction, not an integrated theory, of Goffman's view of the individual.

COMBATING THE 'TOUCHING TENDENCY TO KEEP A PART OF THE WORLD SAFE FROM SOCIOLOGY'

On the last page of 'Role distance' (1961b) Goffman comments on the 'vulgar tendency' of sociologists to attribute the obligatory part of the individual's conduct to the 'profane' sphere of social roles. Meanwhile, 'personal' matters and the warmth, spontaneity and humour of the individual are assigned to a 'sacred' category beyond the remit of sociological analysis. This 'touching tendency to keep a part of the world safe from sociology' (1961b:152) is to be resisted by the role distance concept, devised to capture the manifestations of personal style sociologists attribute to the sacred sphere. Individual idiosyncracies and 'personality' are not allowed to escape Goffman's sociological gaze.

A very general and central theme of Goffman's sociology is its persistent attempt to socially ground the individual, to suggest unenvisaged sociological determinations mainly originating from the interaction order. The 'rules of comingling' comprise a new set of social determinants of individual conduct and experience. The general direction of Goffman's thinking undermines common-sense concepts of a sovereign self and the romantic humanism often associated with it. In identifying the rules and practices of the interaction order he finds a potent sociological determinism in which 'the finger tips of society' (1963b: 53) reach into everyday minutiae. Goffman challenges common understandings about the uniqueness of the individual. He writes: 'the term unique is subject to pressure by maiden social scientists who would make something warm and creative out of it, a something not to be further broken down, at least by sociologists' (1963b: 56). Goffman does not here deny that people have unique selves. But he persists with the sociological question: how is that uniqueness publicly discernible? His answer is that uniqueness is marked by 'identity pegs' such as our knowledge of another's appearance, or our knowledge of their placement in a kinship network and other life history matters. Goffman also states that the individual's uniqueness might refer to the 'core' of their 'being', but he subsequently avoids this meaning, presumably because it lacks empirical reference. 'While it may be true that the individual has a unique self all his own' Goffman writes elsewhere, '*evidence* of this possession is thoroughly a product of joint ceremonial labor' (1967: 85; my emphasis).

Overall, Goffman is not seeking to provide a fully rounded picture of human beings, nor is he engaged in an exposé of people's devices and stratagems. His overriding concern is 'to make the self a visible, sociological phenomenon' (Anderson *et al.* 1985: 152). The visibility of the self is achieved by the serious analytic internalization of G.H. Mead's (1934: 1–8) 'social behaviorism'. Mead held that the proper approach to the self was not the introspectionist approach popular in late nineteenth-century psychology. Rather, he urged that the individual's conduct be inspected for the implications that might be drawn about self.

Goffman imaginatively applies this social behaviourist approach to the study of the interaction order. The result, according to John Helmer (1970), is the depiction of 'the face of the man without qualities' (the allusion is to the title of Robert Musil's novel). Helmer is struck by the way Goffman conceives the individual in 'extrinsic' terms i.e. as composed of properties that require reference to the dynamics of encounters. For example, emotion is seen as an extrinsic property, as a move in a ritual game (1967: 23). More generally Goffman's sociology repeatedly shows how matters that are commonly regarded as personal qualities, properties of the psychology of the individual, can be adequately reconceptualized as part of our socialized competence as interactants, our grasp of the 'proprieties of persondom' (1981a: 94).

This feature of Goffman's sociology bears comparison with continental structuralists' efforts to 'delete' or 'decentre' the subject (Jameson 1976; Gonos 1977; Denzin and Keller 1981). Goffman's explicit response to this interpretation was to distance himself from this brand of structuralism. Yet he acknowledges that 'if the result of my approach can be construed as "decentring" the self, then I am happy to be in the vanguard, providing it is appreciated that this does not mean a lack of interest in the self, merely an effort to approach its figuring from additional directions' (1981b: 62). The problem with traditional sociological analysis is that it 'breaks up the individual into multiple roles but does not suggest that further decimation is required (1974: 516). Such 'decimations', are to be preferred over the 'black box' model favoured by some linguists, who view the individual as an agent who may respond in varying degrees of candour to questions, requests, etc. from information stored inside his/her head (1974: 511–16). Goffman's decimations, in contrast, lean towards what is demonstrably evident in interactional conduct.

However, Goffman's project does require reference to the properties of those who enact that conduct. In the often-quoted words from the 'Introduction' to *Interaction Ritual*:

> I assume that the proper study of interaction is not the individual and his psychology, but rather the syntactical relations among the acts of different persons mutually present to one another. Nonetheless, since it is individual actors who contribute the ultimate materials, it will always be reasonable to ask what general properties they must have if this sort of contribution is to be expected of them. What minimal model of the actor is needed if we are to wind him up, stick him in amongst his fellows, and have an orderly traffic of behavior emerge? What minimal model is required if the student is to anticipate the lines along which an individual, *qua* interactant, and be effective or break down? ... A psychology is necessarily involved, but one stripped and cramped to suit the sociological study of conversation, track meets, banquets, jury trials and street loitering. Not, then, men and their moments. Rather moments and their men. (1967: 2–3)

The psychology that is 'necessarily involved' is thoroughly conditioned by sociological concerns. As critics have noted, this is not a conventional psychology. Goffman recognizes that the only general properties that need to be assigned to the individual are those required for the person to function as an interactant. Once again, Goffman's adaptation of Meadian social behaviourism is apparent. For Mead, the experience of the individual is one 'phase' of social activity, and it arises in the social process (Mead 1934: 7–8). Like Mead, Goffman is interested in what can be inferred about the individual from conduct. A social behaviourist streak also runs through the important remark that 'strips of activity, including the figures who people them' should be treated as a 'single problem for analysis' (1974: 564). For Goffman, just as for Mead, self is to be understood from the vantage of conduct and within an analytical framework that does not radically separate individuals from their conduct.

SELF AND INTERACTION ORDER

Goffman makes surprisingly little use of the identity concepts of *Stigma* in his sociology as a whole. Social identity is produced by social definitions rooted in the society's institutional framework (for example, the valuations implicit in age, class, ethnicity and gender). Ego or felt identity addresses what the person feels about their identity – its subjective side (characteristically, Goffman avoids being drawn into what people say about what they think of their selves by concentrating on the advice given to the stigmatized). Considerations of personal identity loom large in the interaction order, since it is there that social acceptance, character, reputation, composure and the like are enacted. The management of these matters is what Goffman calls 'self-work':

> the individual does not go about merely going about his business. He goes about constrained to sustain a viable image of himself in the eyes of others. Since local circumstances always will reflect upon him, and since these circumstances will vary unexpectedly and constantly, footwork, or rather self work, will be continuously necessary. (1971: 185)

For self work to be successful, the cooperation or at least the forbearance of others is required. The self is here seen as a collaborative achievement, accomplished through face-to-face interaction with others. The role of interactant is, in a sense, additional to whatever social role the individual must play in an encounter (1967: 116, 135). It is also the one role that individuals cannot relinquish at will.

Interaction roles call forth interactional selves. Dramaturgical roles therefore generate 'actors', game roles 'players', and ritual roles 'idols' and 'worshippers'. In practice Goffman frequently merges dramaturgical and game concerns so that the contrasting orientations for interactants reduce to those of information management and ritual. This duality runs through Goffman's sociology, from the dissertation's contrast of tactical and tactful action to the system and ritual constraints of *Forms of Talk* (1981a 14–15m 21).

In examining the flow of information in encounters, Goffman repeatedly emphasizes our capacity to design and control our interactional activity. Such impression management suggests that people present the impression of themselves that they wish others to receive in an attempt to control how those others see them. This emphasis has given rise to the common complaint that Goffman's view of human nature is thoroughly 'Machiavellian' – that he sees people as entirely manipulative, egotistical and cynical beings. Although not without foundation, this interpretation concentrates on only one side of Goffman's thinking about interaction, the informational side, and gives it a predatory gloss. There is another side, centring around Durkheim's notion of ritual, that articulates the various kinds of care and respect (or their opposites: disregard and contempt) that we extend to others. This side presents a very different picture of the interactant's human nature.

Durkheim's thinking about religious ritual is extended to the interactional sphere. Thus, Goffman argues that it is through a multitude of minor acts – addressing someone as 'Mr' or 'Mrs', fetching a chair for a guest, apologizing for late arrival – we show our respect and regard for the feelings of others and the beliefs we hold about the proper treatment of those others. Thus, these minor acts can be seen as 'interaction rituals', through which we affirm the proper character of our relationship to others. Conversely, if we wish to snub or insult others, we do so through the self-same medium of these interaction rituals. Attention to the ritual dimension of interaction leads Goffman (1955) to propose two very basic social rules. For mutually satisfactory interaction to take place, persons must follow a rule of self-respect (they must conduct themselves in a way that shows some pride, dignity and honour) and a rule of considerateness (they must treat others tactfully).

Ritual considerations may impinge on information control. Goffman maintains that our self-presentations have a moral character. That is to say, when we present ourselves in a certain way (e.g. as students), then we have a moral right to expect others (e.g. teachers) to treat us in that way. Rights and duties are part of how we present ourselves to others and their treatment of us. In other words, moral obligations are built right into the detail of interaction. Morality is not something that is diffusely located in 'society' but is rather mediated and renewed in everyday social encounters.

CONCEPTUALIZING THE INTERACTANT

Goffman's abiding fascination for information control and ritual results in a surprisingly rounded account of social being. This account is attuned to both the rational and the emotional elements of interactional conduct, a working through of the classic antinomy between egoism and altruism. It yields two root images of the individual: the calculative, potentially manipulative, egoistic impression manager and games-player (which reaches its apotheosis in *Strategic Interaction*) and the little god who gives as well as gets due deference and considerateness.

Underlying these images of the individual is a general model of the interactant that shifts as Goffman dispenses with his earlier, more anthropocentric views and moves towards a more sociologically consistent conception of self. Three broad stages in this development can be identified: the two selves thesis of *Presentation* and 'On face-work'; the countervailing self of *Asylums;* and the dance of identification view most fully depicted in 'Footing' and 'Radio talk' but which has roots in 'Role distance'.

The two selves thesis

This is Philip Manning's (1992: 44–8) designation for Goffman's conception of self in his early writings. In 'On face-work' and *Presentation* the individual as an interactant is seen in dual terms, as a social product and an agent. As a social product the self is an 'image' that is 'pieced together' from the expressive implications of the encounter (1967: 31) or is a 'character', a 'dramatic effect arising diffusely from a scene that is presented' (1959: 252). As an agent the self is 'a kind of player in a ritual game' (1967: 31) or 'a harried fabricator of impressions involved in the all-too-human task of staging a performance' (1959: 253). The self as image or character is generated as a *product* of interaction, whereas the self as player or performer is the active agent who initiates lines of action in an encounter. For Manning, the first is a performative self, the second a manipulative self. Enough doubts are expressed about dramaturgy in the 1959 edition of *Presentation*, according to Manning, for Goffman to abandon the two selves thesis and to adopt the game metaphor as the dominant model for his inquiries in the 1960s.

The two selves thesis captures important aspects of Goffman's early thinking. However, Manning fails to do justice to its roots and to the subsequent use that Goffman will make of it in the next stage of his thinking, where it serves as a resource for the countervailing self. The two selves thesis effects an interactional application of Mead's famous 'I'/'me' distinction (1934: 173–8). The 'I' is the spontaneous and unselfconscious aspect of the self that is rooted in the psychological and biological impulses of the individual. The 'me' in contrast is a distillation of the responses and attitudes of others to the 'I' and is thoroughly social in nature. The two selves thesis adapts Mead's distinction to the conditions of co-presence. The 'I' becomes the performer, the 'harried fabricator of impressions', a self in tension with the self as socialized character. The performer is grounded in the psychobiological dimension and is the 'human being' of 'variable impulse' portrayed when Goffman identifies:

> a crucial discrepancy between our all-too-human selves and our socialized selves. As human beings we are presumably creatures of variable impulse with moods and energies which change from one moment to the next. As characters put on for an audience, however, we must not be subject to ups and downs … Through social discipline … a mask of manner can be held in place from within. (1959:56–7)

Goffman appears to posit as part of our 'all-too-human selves' something more emotionally grounded than the Meadian 'I', perhaps something more closely akin to Cooley's conception of the 'looking-glass self'. (It is interesting to note that Cooley is referenced on four occasions in *Presentation*; Mead does not merit a single mention.) In common with Cooley, Goffman places great store by the imaginative life of the individual. For example:

> it is known, although perhaps not sufficiently appreciated, that the individual spends a considerable amount of time bathing his wounds in fantasy, imagining the worse things that might befall him, daydreaming about matters sexual, monetary, and so forth. He also rehearses what he will say when the time comes and privately formulates what he should have said after it has come and gone … We are the vehicles of society; but we are also overheated engines prone to keep firing even though the ignition is turned off. (1974: 551–2)

The performer's fantasies, daydreams, variable moods and energies and the like must be disciplined and channelled for euphoric interaction to take place. In the next stage of Goffman's thinking about self, the performer is transformed into what Edwin Lemert (1972) calls 'the countervailing self'.

The countervailing self

'A chief concern', Goffman says of *Asylums*, is 'to develop a sociological version of the structure of the self' (1961a: xiii). However the use of the singular is apt to mislead, for there are two conceptions of the self that repeatedly surface in *Asylums*. One is the self personified in the total institution's definitions of appropriate role behaviour for the inmate; the other is a self that resists these definitions: the countervailing self. These two conceptions represent a transformation of the character and performer concepts of self to the organizational context of the total institution. While Goffman's ethnography focuses on face-to-face interaction, his analysis shows a strong recognition of organizational constraint on who and what the patient should be. All organizations define a person's self in terms of the obligations and expectations attached to organizational roles. But the 'encompassing tendencies' of the total institution take the organizational determination of self to an extreme, since they attempt to exercise control over every significant part of the inmate's life. They are 'the forcing houses for extreme persuasion; each is a natural experiment on what can be done to the self' (p. 12).

The total institution treats the inmate as its 'raw material', to be excluded from civil society and reorganized. However, the organizational determination of self is seldom wholly successful, since inmates protect themselves from psychological assault by seeking out unofficial bases of self-identification. The basic theme of *Asylums* – the struggle between the organizationally-determined self and the countervailing self – is introduced in the first paper and developed with reference to the mental patient in the next two. Consequently, the inmate is only partly defined in terms of the organization's expectations. Seen in the full round of inmate activity, s/he is also portrayed as declining some of these expectations.

The analysis of the countervailing and the organizationally-ascribed self is developed, somewhat confusingly in places, in 'The moral career of the mental patient'. Goffman's broad argument is that most patients are unwillingly or unwittingly hospitalized, victims of an 'alienative coalition' (1961a: 137) that includes those kin and friends who should protect their interests. Once hospitalized the patient is obliged to come to terms with the ward system and the implications it holds for his/her new self. The paper concludes with a somewhat contradictory analysis of the self. The dominant conception is of a self determined and constituted by organizational demands:

> The self, then, can be seen as something that resides in the arrange-
> ments prevailing in a social system for its members. The self in

this sense is not a property of the person to whom it is attributed, but dwells rather in the pattern of social control that is exerted in connection with the person himself and those around him. This special kind of institutional arrangement does not so much support the self as constitute it. (1961a:168)

But there is also a countervailing self that plays 'shameless games'. The inmate learns to appreciate how self is 'something outside oneself that can be constructed, lost and rebuilt all with great speed and some equanimity', that it is 'not a fortress but a small open city', that the construction and destruction of self on the wards is a 'shameless game' (p.165).

Inmates insult staff or practise the 'marriage moratorium' in the knowledge that these activities will have no significant or lasting implications for the self. This countervailing self seems to exist in spite of the self-defining implications of the social arrangements that apply to the mental patient. The countervailing self is not constituted by social arrangements but apparently emerges as a result of the experiences undergone in the pre-patient and in-patient phases. It is the cumulative consequence of the train of experiences suffered by the patient: betrayal by the inmate's intimates and kin, mortification of self upon entry to the mental hospital, and the subsequent discrediting of every attempt to sustain a viable self. The sum consequence is that the patient comes to appreciate how a viable self is built out of social arrangements. The patient becomes morally loosened or fatigued because s/he senses the essential arbitrariness of these social arrangements.

The secondary adjustments described in the 'Underlife' paper are the key expressions of the countervailing self. The 'recalcitrance' that secondary adjustments evidence, Goffman concludes, 'is not an incidental mechanism of defense but rather an essential constituent of the self' (p. 319). The view of the individual as being 'to himself what his place in an organization defines him to be' is compromised whenever close observation of any element of social life is undertaken since 'we always find the individual employing methods to keep some distance, some elbow room, between himself and that with which others assume he should be identified'. And again, 'in all situations actually studied the participant has erected defenses against his social bondedness' (p. 319). The countervailing self is so universal a feature of social life that Goffman argues that the individual can be defined:

for sociological purposes, as a stance-taking entity, a something that takes up a position somewhere between identification with an organization and opposition to it ... It is thus against something that the self can emerge. (1961a: 320)

The last paragraph of the paper expands this view:

Without something to belong to, we have no stable self, and yet total commitment and attachment to any social unit implies a kind of selflessness. Our sense of being a person can come from being drawn into a wider social unit; our sense of selfhood can arise through the little ways in which we resist the pull. Our status is backed by the solid buildings of the world, while our sense of personal identity often resides in the cracks. (1961a: 320)

Goffman intends the argument to apply both to mental patients and those in 'free society'. However, the two views of the self offered in *Asylums* are not well integrated: what is the relation of the countervailing self that 'resides in the cracks' to the self determined by meeting the obligations of organizations and other social entities? For a more cogent statement, we must turn to 'Role distance' (in Goffman 1961b).

That cogency derives from the interactional frame of reference that Goffman adopts to criticize traditional sociological conceptions of social role. These conceive social role as the normatively determined orientations and actions of an actor occupying a given status in a 'patterned interactive relationship' (Parsons 1951: 25). This theory implies that a self awaits the individual taking a role. Conformity with the demands of the role gives the individual a particular 'me': 'in the language of Kenneth Burke, doing is being' (1961b: 88). One of the problems with this view is that it assumes that the actor will automatically become attached to the role and the 'me' that goes with it. It neglects 'the many roles that persons play with detachment, shame or resentment' (p. 90). However, by taking the 'more atomistic frame of reference' (p. 95) of the 'situated activity system' or encounter the 'complexities of concrete conduct' can be 'examined instead of by-passed'.

In the encounter the individual takes a 'situated role' with its accompanying 'situated self' (p. 97). When the encounter is taken as an analytical frame of reference the 'problem of expression' (pp. 99–105) can be addressed: individuals may not merely enact situated role expectations but may 'play at' rather than 'play' the role; they may 'break role' or 'go out of role' ('brown studies', etc.); and they may 'style' the role in their own way. The possibilities the problem of expression opens leads Goffman to propose two kinds of involvement: 'role embracement', where the individual is attached to the role and spontaneously involved in it and 'role distance', those often humorous or playful actions that 'constitute a wedge between the individual and his role, between doing and being'. Role distance concerns these forms of '"effectively" expressed pointed separateness' between the individual and his/her role and serve not to deny the role, but rather the self it implies (p. 108). Goffman suggests that what the individual does in taking role distance is not an expression of their essential self or uniqueness as a human being. Rather, the individual invokes another, situationally-irrelevant source of self-identification – a 'negational self' (Chriss 1999) – such as the diffuse roles of 'man' and 'woman' in the case of sexual banter between surgeons and nurses during surgical operations.

The concept of role distance combats 'the touching tendency to keep a part of the world safe from sociology' by providing a sociological account of those items of conduct commonly regarded as expressions of the person's individuality. It is also instructive to compare Goffman's treatment of individuality with that of Dahrendorf (1973). In 'Homo sociologicus' Dahrendorf is disquietened by the disparity between the 'glass men' of sociological role theory and the lively individuals of our everyday experience. How are they to be reconciled? Dahrendorf offers two solutions. The first draws upon an idea from Robert Musil's 1952 novel, *The Man Without Qualities*. Musil postulates a 'tenth character', 'the passive fantasy of unfilled spaces' that permits human beings everything except the need to take seriously our characters as determined by our roles. The second solution derives from Kant, who distinguished between the individual as an occupant of the sensible world who was knowable, empirical, determined and unfree, and the individual as occupant of the intelligible world who was unknowable, transcendental, undetermined and free (Dahrendorf 1973: 56–64). Both of Dahrendorf's solutions are extra-sociological, metaphysical. Goffman, on the other hand, presents a solution to Dahrendorf's dilemma from within a sociological framework.

The concept of role distance allows Goffman to refine his initial notion of the self as performer. With it he can cast off anthropomorphic allusions to 'all-too human-selves' and sociologically locate individuality in situated or interactional roles that are responsive to the organization of face-to-face interaction. But role distance itself proves a transitional concept. The depiction of persons as a 'simultaneous multiplicity of selves' engaged in a 'dance of identification' (1961b: 144) paves the way to his late view of the self as a constellation of interaction contingencies and frame functions.

The stance taking entity's dance of identification

Throughout *Frame Analysis*, Goffman continues to prod common-sense views about individuality and personal identity. The section, 'The human being' (1974: 293–300) questions the common-sense view of a durable, abiding, 'perduring self' expressed in the person's acts. Goffman doubts that any of these acts provide a glimpse of what the person really is. The importance of these acts is that they provide other people with a 'sense' (p. 298) of what the person is like behind actions and roles. We cannot presume that these 'gleanings' about the person will point to a stable, consistent image of the 'perduring self'. That self is only an operating fiction sustained by our beliefs about the individual personality. So a witticism does not 'disclose or conceal the perduring nature of its maker'. Instead, its function is to display the maker's possession of witty sentiments that run no deeper than the situated role the witticism generates. Moreover, opportunities for these expressions of personal identity are not randomly distributed through social life: they are responsive to social occasions and frames, which secure their situational appropriateness.

In Goffman's later works, dualist conceptions of self as character and as performer, and organizationally-determined and countervailing selves are abandoned in favour of a flatter view of self, regarded as 'not an entity half-concealed behind events, but a changeable formula for managing oneself during them' (1974: 573). Self is no longer seen as a hidden manipulator or an insurrectionary against the social order. Instead Goffman develops his earlier notion of the self as 'stance-taking entity' and asks how these stances are manifested in the processes of ordinary conduct. The dance of identification earlier associated with role distance now comes to be seen as an endemic feature of a variety of forms of talk: conversational interaction, lecturing, radio announcing and also the 'fresh talk' we take to occupy much of our everyday life. But instead of speaking anthropomorphically of a 'multiplicity of selves', or imprecisely through role concepts (including, presumably, his own earlier notions of role distance and situated roles), Goffman now deploys production format, participation framework and in 'Radio talk', the concept of 'frame space' (1981a: 230). The point of these distinctions is to accommodate the changes in footing and multiple voices that make up the shifting alignments that occur as individuals respond to local circumstances. Self is nothing more than the capacity to manage these alignments.

ASSESSING GOFFMAN'S INDIVIDUAL

Seen sociologically up close, Goffman averred, the individual becomes a 'blur'. Part of Goffman's project was to identify the constituents of this blur. Among the terms he used to sociologically specify the individual were the concepts of social, personal and ego identities; actor, player, worshipper; interactant, self, person; performer, character; production format, participation framework. Four overlapping areas of criticism and debate about Goffman's formulations have emerged:

1   The two selves thesis of *Presentation* seems to advance a hidden real
    self who is an immoral manipulator of appearances (Cuzzort 1969;
    Gouldner 1970). Whether interactants universally possess such an
    awareness has been disputed (Messinger *et al.* 1962; Tseëlon 1992).
    Whether such manipulation is a 'bad thing' depends very much upon the
    value positions being taken. These judgements are likely to be variable
    and contextual matters. In some circumstances, positive valuation may
    be placed on adept opportunism (Lyman and Scott 1970: 69).
2   The dramaturgical self is seen to be morally ambiguous and
    phenomenologically incoherent (Wilshire 1982; Ostrow 1996). It
    unreasonably liquidates self into role-playing, as against an older and
    more satisfactory conception of self in which the Aristotelian virtues
    are central (MacIntyre 1981). It fails to posit genuine agency and does
    not address the persistence and continuity of the self through time,
    which leads to an incapacity to explain moral behaviour (Miller 1984,
    1986).
3   The construal of self in extrinsic, interactional terms (face, footing and
    the like), as an interactional functionary bereft of a 'substantival self'
    (Weigert 1975) and interior specifications, also has been differently
    valued. Some see Goffman's focus on 'moments and their men' with
    its analytical elevation of situations over personal qualities and inner
    lives as a sociological advance (Helmer 1970; Lyman and Scott,
    1970: 20; Gonos 1977, 1980). Others (e.g. Sennett 1977) argue that
    it leaves us with an impoverished view of the self or one that requires
    supplementation by a fuller account of human subjectivity.
4   Some ethnomethodologists (notably Schegloff 1988) hold that sociology
    has no disciplinary interest in self, even Goffman's interactional version,
    which is held to divert attention away from the 'moments' towards the
    'men' (and women). The discovery of the syntax of interaction in this
    view is best advanced by approaches like conversation analysis that
    do not require a notion of self as part of its analytical apparatus.

Many of these criticisms raise questions about the nature of human
motivation, social action and morality of the kind sometimes subsumed
under the heading of 'philosophical anthropology'. Characteristically,
Goffman was not interested in these larger questions, nor did he intervene
in debates about his models of human nature. His interest remained focused
on the relation of self to the interaction order. Here, as Anne Rawls (1987)
suggests, the expressive capacities and ritual roles of the self set technical
and moral constraints on the organization of the interaction order.

   A critical task for Goffman's sociology was the development of
sociological conceptions of the individual as an *interactant*. A major theme

running through Goffman's various formulations of the interactant is a resistance to simple determinisms, whether these are believed to emanate from role theory or sequential organization. Most fundamentally, the interactant's self is a 'stance-taking entity', as is evident in the underlife and role distance essays on, but which reaches back to the early conception of the performer and is traceable right through to the dissection of the varying agents (animator, author and principal) embedded in talk's 'production format'. Few sociologists have followed Goffman's abiding concern with the interactivity of the interactant (but see Travers 1992). However, Goffman does not, with his preoccupation with the responsiveness of the interactant, lose sight of wider organizational and institutional determinants of self. This lends Goffman's account an unusual complexity. For these reasons it is not surprising that Cahill (1998) regards Goffman's sociology as pivotal in contemporary attempts to develop Mauss's project of a sociology of the person.

In addition, Goffman clearly recognizes the importance of embodiment in his conception of the interactant. His sociology treats embodied states in a consistently social manner. Thus the cardinal emotion of embarrassment (Schudson 1984) concentrates on the consequences of its interactional manifestations, not its function as a sign of the individual's inward states. Response cries are not expressions of unsocialized feelings but have a display function, announcing the interactant's continuing adherence to a norm of controlled alertness (1981a: 78–123). Genderisms display not the essential biological natures of men and women but the culturally conventional assumptions about how those natures are allowed to become evident in social situations (1979: 3–8). Goffman shows how there is very little that is natural, and much that is social, about human expression. It is not surprising, therefore, that proponents of the sociology of the body (e.g. Turner 1984; Shilling 1993; Crossley 1995) have found in Goffman a rich resource that they continue to mine.

8
Methods and Textuality

'A MODEST BUT PERSISTENT ANALYTICITY'

Goffman's sociology has a look and a tone all of its own. Resisting easy categorization, it quickly became a source of puzzlement and misunderstanding. Commentators have remarked that Goffman was too empirical in his preoccupations to be considered a theorist, yet too theoretical to be regarded as simply an ethnographer. The absence of a single recognizable method in Goffman's writings lies at the heart of many misgivings expressed by his critics The distinctiveness of his approach – what has been called its signature style – has attracted criticism in almost equal measure to admiration. At its baldest, critics complain first, that Goffman's sociology lacks a method, and second, that it fails to offer genuine theories or explanations of social life.

Sociologists encounter difficulties in following in Goffman's footprints, it is said, because Goffman lacked a 'method', in the sense of an explicit set of reproducible and teachable procedures for collecting and analysing sociological data. Goffman told his readers relatively little about how he gathered his data and selected the examples that figure in his analyses. Thus complaints accumulate around the disparate data sources found in Goffman's work and the absence of reliable procedures for analysing the minutiae of interaction. For example Gamson (1975) applauds Goffman's inventiveness and perspicacity but worries that his sociological practice cannot be taught to students. From a very different sociological perspective Schegloff (1988) maintains that Goffman manages to convey the illusion of working in a densely empirical way without ever producing the substantial ethnographic detail needed to warrant his interpretations. Goffman's 'sociology by epitome', Schegloff suggests, relies upon its readers to supply the missing detail from their commonsense cultural knowledge. In sum, Goffman's analyses seem so closely enmeshed in their author's evident insightfulness and the ingenuity of his writing that it is difficult to justify the appellation of 'method' in any of its conventional senses.

A second broad complaint is that Goffman fails to produce any genuine theories or explanations of social life. This takes two versions, one social scientific and one philosophical. In the first version Goffman does not meet the accepted criteria of fully-fledged theory and hypothetico-deductive explanation characteristic of social science. Adjudged against orthodox social scientific criteria, Goffman fails to present his ideas as a set of interrelated propositions that causally explain social phenomena. Bernard Meltzer and his colleagues aptly sum up this line of criticism, even as they note Goffman's alternative qualities:

> We find in his work no explicit theory, but a plausible and loosely organized frame of reference; little interest in explanatory schemes, but masterful descriptive analysis; virtually no accumulated evidence, but illuminating allusions, impressions, anecdotes, and illustrations; few formulations of empirically testable propositions, but innumerable provocative insights. In addition, we find an insufficiency of qualifications and reservations, so that the limits of generalization are not indicated.
>
> (Meltzer *et al.* 1975: 70–1)

Philosophers have also criticized Goffman for failing to provide adequate explanations of social life. Some consider that there is nothing for Goffman to explain since as members of society we already have perfectly adequate explanations of the matters Goffman describes, available to us as part of our commonsense cultural knowledge. Frank Cioffi (2000) pungently expresses this view, claiming that there are no real discoveries in Goffman's sociology, merely a rearrangement of what we already know, presented in an obfuscating terminology that panders to the human need for a synoptic view of life's petty difficulties.

All these criticisms entertain theoretical expectations that exceed Goffman's quite modest ambitions for his own work. They make demands at variance with how Goffman saw his analytical task. He saw his work as fundamentally exploratory in character, a preliminary to the kinds of sociological theorizing and investigation the critics faulted him for not providing, not a substitute for that serious, systematic work. The concessions he implicitly requests are those to be allowed to the 'student' working in a context of discovery, seeking to develop his science not simply apply it. Goffman agrees that his work is 'full of unverified assertions' that can only be established 'by systematic empirical research'. But Goffman refuses to see this as a shortcoming since 'a loose speculative approach to a fundamental area of conduct is better than a rigorous blindness to it' (1963a: 4–5).

At its simplest, he was following in Simmel's footsteps, seeking to abstract the forms or basic structuring principles of social life and identify them conceptually. Goffman's analytic focus on the interaction order was more specific than Simmel's, and he was more systematic than his acknowledged master in categorizing the features to which he wished to draw our attention. He did not want to be thought 'merely' a brilliant observer or sociological impressionist, one of the fates that befell Simmel's more fragmentary approach. In common with Simmel, Goffman regarded his project as exploratory and provisional in character. The sociological mapping of the interaction order could be best achieved by articulating the concepts that identified the outstanding features of the new terrain. Hence a large portion of Goffman's sociology consists of concepts he has devised, or has borrowed or adapted from others, which are then connected together into conceptual frameworks that are organized around an analytical theme: the main forms of face-work and how they are enacted, how members of teams collaborate to produce performances, how normal appearances are sustained and threatened, and so on. Each concept is illustrated with examples designed to instantiate the point the concept makes. Goffman drew his illustrations from a wide range of sources: his own ethnographic fieldwork, other social science studies, literary sources, the *faits divers* of newspaper columns, observations of conduct he had personally witnessed. These illustrations, as we shall see, play a vital role in Goffman's sociology. They are never mere padding, usually very carefully selected and rarely banal as illustrations of the concept they instantiate. The development of these richly illustrated conceptual frameworks is the analytical core of Goffman's 'method'.

Goffman was never seduced by the blandishments of theory talk in sociology. His cautious attitude towards theoretical ambition was in place long before deconstruction and disquisitions around the postmodern made scepticism about theory fashionable. In the 1950s Goffman lampooned the hasty interdisciplinary theorizing that attempted to marry sociological interests to psychiatric ones as 'one part taffy and three parts corn flakes' (1957b: 201). A quarter of a century later he was no more optimistic, remarking 'it is our easy use of the term "theory" everywhere in sociology, not our not having any, that marks us off from the disciplines that do'

(1981c: 4). Goffman's aims were always more limited and circumscribed. He doubted the value of grand and middle range theory, recommending something more basic, 'a modest but persistent analyticity: frameworks of the lower range':

> I believe that the provision of a single conceptual distinction, if it orders, and illuminates, and reflects delight in the contours of our data, can warrant our claim to be students of society. And surely, if we can't uncover processes, mechanisms, structures and variables that cause others to see what they hadn't seen or connect what they hadn't put together, then we have failed critically. (1981c: 4)

Conceptual work was important for Goffman not only because it ordered and illuminated but also made linkages that participants did not themselves always see or fully appreciate. His concepts provided new ways of seeing interactional matters that were often taken for granted or out of participants' ordinary awareness.

For Goffman, the development of the sociology of the interaction order depended on conceptual work of a special kind: the assembly of thickly illustrated conceptual frameworks. It is the detail that Goffman packs into his frameworks that distinguishes them from those of Talcott Parsons, who in the early 1950s was also proposing that sociology might be significantly advanced by a conceptual strategy. Parsons wanted a single categorial scheme that would offer a universal language for the analytic description of social structures and processes. Goffman's approach was more pragmatic and resulted in a multiplicity of conceptual frameworks, a far cry from the unity towards which Parsons aspired.

Goffman was against narrow conceptions of how sociology could be scientific. He maintained that there is no single way to do scientific sociology, no royal road to a science of social life, and certainly not one of positivist, quantitative stripe. But Goffman was far from being anti-scientific. For example, in a 1964 conference discussion, he disagrees with the easy distinction between 'scientific statements and other kinds'. He says:

> I would not phrase the problem that way. There are statements which involve a few clear-cut sets of facts and which are conveniently testable, if not already tested. There are other statements based on a large number of heterogeneous unorganized observations, and not easily subject to confirmation or disconfirmation. However, while these kinds of statement differ, I think they can both be made in a scientific spirit.
>
> (Goffman 1964: 288)

A scientific temper remained a significant dimension of how he saw his project. In his Presidential Address to the American Sociological Association he teased readers about the importance of keeping 'faith with the spirit of natural sciences ... seriously kidding ourselves that our rut has a forward direction' (1983a: 2). At the same time, he also cautioned professional sociologists not to so fetishize science as to attain the high level of trained incompetence found in parts of psychology. Goffman concluded that same paper with a reminder that modern sociology's 'systematic', 'meticulous', and 'unfettered, unsponsored inquiry' was a historically recent and hard-won achievement. Sociologists, he seemed to say, have no need of any particular conception of science, but *some* notion of the rigour associated with scientificity must inform their work. Goffman was for science but against scientism.

Goffman's thinking seems to anticipate Feyerabend's thesis that science has no single set of overarching and always-applicable rules of procedure, so that in any final sense, 'anything goes'. Recalling their conversations from the early 1950s, Howard S. Becker (2003) maintained that Goffman 'felt very strongly that you could not elaborate any useful rules of procedure for doing field research and that if you attempted to do that, people would misinterpret what you had written, do it (whatever *it* was) wrong, and then blame you for the resulting mess' (Becker 2003: 660). Goffman's 'principled indifference' to articulating rules of method perhaps explains why his methodological comments appear only as fugitive remarks in the prefaces and introductions of his books. They are never given the conventional social scientific status of a separate chapter or an appendix. With these provisos in place we can go on to ask: what methods does Goffman use to collect his empirical materials? How does he produce concepts and frameworks on the basis of this data? What are the characteristic ways in which Goffman presents his analyses?

NATURALISTIC OBSERVATION

Goffman trusted direct observation of social life and was wary of sole dependence on verbal testimony as a basis for sociological analysis, evident in sociology's heavy reliance on the interview. This is conveyed very clearly in Goffman's 1974 talk on method, later published from a bootlegged tape: 'I don't give hardly any weight to what people say, but I try to triangulate what they're saying with events' (1989: 131). Such 'naturalistic study' required observing social conduct as it occurs, in its natural social setting. It might involve sustained spells of fieldwork using the method of participant observation, but naturalistic observation also covers the many chance observations Goffman witnessed in his daily life that find their way into his writing. Naturalistic observation was overwhelmingly Goffman's own favoured research method and the primary approach he urged his students to adopt. The method and its rationale are neatly summed up in his much-quoted statement:

> any group of persons – prisoners, primitives, pilots or patients – develop a life of their own that becomes meaningful, reasonable and normal once you get close to it ... a good way to learn about any of these worlds is to submit oneself in the company of the members to the daily round of petty contingencies to which they are subject. (1961a: ix-x)

From his PhD dissertation on, where he aimed to be more an 'observant participant' than a 'participating observer' (1953a: 2), Goffman recommends careful scrutiny of people's conduct in its normal, natural setting. Observing what people do in the artificial situation of the experimental psychology laboratory will not do. Naturalistic observation does not exclude talking to people about their conduct, but it goes beyond simply interviewing people because ethnographic data are best gathered:

> by subjecting yourself, your own body and your own personality, and your own social situation, to the set of contingencies that play upon a set of individuals, so that you can physically and ecologically penetrate their circle of response to their social situation, or their work situation, or their ethnic situation ... so that you are close to them while they are responding to what life does to them. (1989: 125)

Goffman's argument is that there is an embodied basis to the empathetic understanding that participant observers seek (Charmaz 2004). That understanding comes about because 'you've been taking the same crap they've been taking' (1989: 125). His thoroughly unsentimental approach is often thought to tilt his ethnography towards a non-interventionist, fly-on-the-wall observational stance. At the extreme, this stance might place him in a position analogous to the war photographer making pictures of atrocities (consider, for example, Goffman's report of incidents of patient misconduct; 1963a: 207–8). Goffman was never under the illusion that the style of fieldwork he recommended was anything but a tough discipline to undertake. Nor were the moral ambiguities of the method lost on Goffman. After all, he began his 1974 talk by describing it as work 'done by two kinds of "finks"' (1989: 125), the police and ethnographers. If Goffman had little to say on fieldwork ethics, it was perhaps because of his acute sense of the possibilities of betrayal inhering in fieldwork practice.

Goffman's experience as a participant observer included three substantial stints of fieldwork: in Shetland between 1949–51, reported in his PhD dissertation; at St. Elizabeths Hospital between 1955–6, reported in *Asylums*; and in the casinos of Reno and Las Vegas, which featured varying kinds of participation, beginning around 1958 and continuing through to the mid-1960s, and which was only partially reported in 'Where the action is'. In addition he undertook some shorter periods of fieldwork: first, around 1954–5, at a research mental hospital in the District of Columbia area (the basis of 'Deference and demeanor'), second, at the surgical facility at St. Elizabeths and, in the late 1950s, at Herrick Memorial Hospital, Berkeley (providing the surgical examples in 'Role distance') and third, some brief observations and an interview with a DJ on a classical radio station (one source of the illustrations in 'Radio talk').

Goffman extended the method of naturalistic observation into his own everyday life. He was adept at utilizing snatches of overheard conversation and little scenes he had personally witnessed as source materials. Goffman treated his own daily life as a research setting that constantly furnished him with instances of co-present conduct to ponder and analyse. In so doing he demonstrated that one did not need special training or privileged access to a group of people in order to do ethnographic work. He expanded not just the scope but also the sensibility of ethnographic vision.

But he recognized also that one person's experience, while a valid source of sociological insight, did not provide the breadth of examples to allow him to make the wide-ranging comparisons needed to uncover pattern in social life. Goffman's extensive use of personal accounts, newspaper stories and other documentary materials, are sometimes understood as stand-ins for observational work. In the preface to *Presentation* Goffman recognized the 'mixed status' of his 'illustrative materials':

> some are taken from respectable researches where qualified generalizations are given regarding reliably recorded regularities; some are taken from informal memoirs written by colorful people; many fall in between. (1959: xi)

In *Stigma* there is much use of first-person accounts set out in self-help manuals, autobiographies and advice books. The pictorial matter of *Gender Advertisements* was extracted from a much larger collection of advertising images. The memoirs of staff serving in the intelligence services figures in *Strategic Interaction*. 'Radio talk' includes transcribed data from records of 'bloopers'. Many of his books draw upon excerpts from novels, newspaper clippings and etiquette books. On the one hand, some of these documents provide first-person accounts that provide insight into the person's situation and experiences. On the other hand, Goffman sometimes seems to want them to serve as proxy observational data, even though they are at one step removed from whatever naturalistic observation might reveal. Commentators have been uneasy about Goffman's apparent indifference to the diversity of these materials, which are all grist to Goffman's analytic mill. Questions about the adequacy of these sources of data raise wider questions about the primacy Goffman accords conceptual articulation. Three issues will be reviewed: how Goffman produces his concepts; the role of the data Goffman uses to illustrate his concepts; and the overall development of his conceptual schemes.

CONCEPTUAL WORK

Concept production

For Goffman even more than for Simmel, the production of formal concepts becomes an instrument of sociological discovery. Goffman poured scorn on advocates of supposedly more rigorous experimental methods for mistakenly assuming that 'if you go through the motions attributable to science then science will result. But it hasn't' (1971: xviii). However, his remarks seem less motivated by wholesale rejection of quantitative, empiricist conceptions of sociology as they are by a recognition that such methods, when followed unreflectively, can subvert the process of scientific discovery:

> Concepts have not emerged that reorder our view of social activity. Frameworks have not been established into which a continuously larger number of facts can be placed. Understanding of ordinary behavior has not accumulated; distance has. (1971: xviii)

The work of a discovering science, for Goffman, centres on developing new concepts that permit new ways of seeing.

Goffman's Chicagoan emphasis on the centrality of naturalistic observation ensured that there was never a risk of his conceptual work degenerating into scholastic analytics. Goffman maintained that his work contained a strong inductive component, in that concepts were formulated in light of fieldwork and other kinds of data-gathering. Goffman denied that data were supplied simply to illustrate ideas arrived at earlier. There was an interaction between a developing conceptual organization and the facts collected via fieldwork (1953a: 4, 9). In a 1980 interview, he says that he uses the data he has collected in an unsystematic way, 'as a check upon just making wild imputations' (Verhoeven 1993: 340) about conduct.

This component of Goffman's method approximates to the method of analytic induction that was in vogue in Chicago circles in the 1940s and 1950s, and which was later developed by Glaser and Strauss (1967) as 'grounded theory'. In the method of analytic induction working hypotheses are corrected by deviant cases and are refined and reformulated until a universal relationship is established (Becker (1953) on marijuana users offers a classic example of the method). Goffman did seem to take the analysis of deviant cases seriously. This is apparent in *Gender Advertisements*, where examples of gender displays that contradict the dominant pattern are identified by a black border. However, Goffman was unwilling to characterize his work as analytic induction. Given his 'principled indifference' to questions of method, and also his (1957d) sceptical review of Cressey's famed study of embezzlement that is often taken as an exemplar of analytic induction, this is not surprising. At best, elements of the method may have influenced his ways of working, but he was never an adherent to its principles.

Adjudged in terms a neighbouring methodological approach, grounded theory, Goffman again shows superficial similarities but again no real thoroughgoing resemblance. Among ethnographically-oriented researchers in a range of disciplines grounded theory has had major impact. Barney Glaser and Anselm Strauss (1967) want sociologists to systematically discover and generate theory from their data. Glaser and Strauss note many virtues in Goffman's approach. They see *Stigma* as an attempt to generate grounded theory from a wide range of substantive areas and data sources. They applaud Goffman's readiness to organize 'commonalities' across seemingly non-comparable groups, his success in developing analytic, sensitizing concepts, and the reasoned manner in which his analytic frameworks are developed. But Goffman fails to inform readers about precisely how his concepts have been generated from his fieldwork or from his other data sources. Grounded theory seeks to make explicit and systematic the process whereby concepts and generalizations are generated, and Goffman is signally silent on these matters. Goffman's concepts emerge in what grounded theory might regard as a sociological version of the immaculate conception. Glaser and Strauss note Goffman's dependence upon the technique of 'exampling', his use of 'circumstantial' rather than 'theoretical' sampling and conclude that the degree to which Goffman's theorizing is grounded in their sense is problematic.

In sum, Goffman's concepts are not merely 'mentalistic adumbrations' (as he mockingly characterized his own efforts). They emerge out of an interaction with an undisclosed collection of data. Does it matter that Goffman's processes of concept formation are hidden from view? There does need to be 'a check upon just making wild imputations' but whether the detailed history of concept formation would add much to the reader's confidence in Goffman's formulations is debatable. That confidence perhaps depends more on how the examples that Goffman cites actually work to illustrate his concepts.

Concepts and illustrative materials

The devising of concepts to name features of the interaction order – 'nomination' (Jameson 1976: 127) – was one of Goffman's most remarkable talents. He gave names to new social objects: withs, civil inattention, response cries, and so on. For all his advocacy of naturalistic observation, he is never satisfied with 'mere' ethnography. Goffman constantly generalizes beyond his ethnographic particulars, using the data he has collected to provide illustrations for the current analytic theme he is developing. Goffman's interest was never to provide the vivid detail of a case study but rather to act, as he once put it, like a 'one-armed botanist' (quoted in Strong 1983) needful of instances to fill the categories of his taxonomies. These classifications were intended to identify the stable patterns he detected in the interaction order.

The component parts of Goffman's taxonomies are 'sensitizing concepts' designed, as Blumer (1969) pointed out, to alert the sociologist to general features of a phenomenon rather than to provide very specific benchmarks. Sensitizing concepts are thus neatly tailored to the needs of an exploratory enterprise like Goffman's. Concepts, of course, are not theories and so cannot be straightforwardly falsified. As Lewis Coser (1956) noted, 'they are apt or inept, clear or vague, fruitful or useless'. Quoting Merton he continues, 'they are the tools designed to capture relevant aspects of reality and thus "constitute the definitions (or prescriptions) or what is to be observed"'. Concepts simply function to tell us what is there. They are the bedrock on which shifting and developing hypotheses and theories can be constructed.

Goffman's concepts about the forms of interaction cannot be falsified, since all they do is point to the existence of phenomena like face-saving practices or moral careers. The role of the examples Goffman provides to illustrate his concepts is to validate the concept by giving it some empirical reference, to show us what actual instances of the concept look like. In this way the illustrations alert us to the potential utility of a concept. The illustrations are a first and elementary type of testing. At times Goffman underplays his hand, or perhaps engages in misdirection, with repeated disclaimers about the deficiencies of his data (e.g. 1959: xi; 1963a: 5; 1971: xvii; 1974: 14; 1979: 26) that seem to assume that illustrations must always meet the criteria of evidence. Goffman is nearer the mark when he writes of his illustrations as 'a cross between an *experimentum crucim* and a sideshow' (1974: 14). Illustrations do not prove anything except show an instance of the concept's application. The question of how useful or fruitful a concept is can only be settled by further investigations that apply it to different social settings. Goffman thus states that *Presentation* might serve as 'a guide worth testing in case-studies of institutional social life' (1959: xii). We might speak of 'testing out' rather than testing in its more usual (hypothesis–testing) sense. Researchers who employ Goffman's concepts test them out by showing their scope, ubiquity, empirical necessity, precision, etc. in the areas of empirical investigation to which they have been applied. It is to this work that we must turn in order to find out how apt, clear, fruitful or otherwise Goffman's concepts may be, for as he once put it, 'none of the concepts elaborated [here] may have a future' (1981a: 1). Only uptake by other researchers will determine the utility of the concept for sociological inquiry.

Development of conceptual frameworks

Why did Goffman choose to proliferate conceptual frameworks without ever seeking to consolidate them? His characteristic tendency to begin each paper and book anew, his constant fresh starts, irritated even those readers who appreciated the detail of his sociological labours. Why did Goffman signally fail to trace the links between his present concerns and previous work? These irritations could be coupled with other apparent methodological delinquencies. They include his sometimes wayward handling of concepts, such as his use of different terms for the same concept, and those instances where 'other people's concepts have their names changed' (Phillips 1983: 114). Goffman seemed to treat diverse data sources (first-hand observations, first-person accounts, extracts from fiction, recollected conversations, and taped and transcribed conversational data) as if they were all of a piece. It all adds up, apparently, to methodological negligence on a formidable scale, giving succour to those who insist that Goffman lacked a procedure to direct his analyses.

Perhaps the best attempt to defend Goffman against these charges is Robin Williams' (1988) analysis of Goffman's methods. Williams proposes that the ostensible flaws of Goffman's methods (his persistent restarts, the problems in concept and data management outlined above) can be more positively seen as part of a logic of discovery. Williams' argument shows how Goffman uses these putative faults to explore and consolidate a stable conceptual core for the study of interaction. Williams draws upon W.W. Baldamus' notions of 'articulation' and 'double fitting'. These terms identify 'an analytical process whereby an initially vague and vacillating image of a complex framework is perpetually refined so as to produce an increasingly definite and stable structure' (Williams 1988: 74). Seen thus,

Goffman's sociology is not an aimless collection of inventive insights but is in a real sense progressive. By means of 'innumerable trial and error actions' Goffman refines his conceptual frameworks so that they become more general and able to incorporate a growing range of facts. Goffman explored the vulnerabilities of his favoured metaphors (dramaturgy, ritual and game) constantly searching for counter-examples to refine his frameworks. Goffman's remarkable facility for devising fresh conceptual frameworks is thus the means through which he could continuously cultivate and update his ideas in a principled manner and thus maximize the opportunities for conceptual development and sociological discovery. Even fictional examples have a role to play in this process, for they allow a mapping of concepts in a realm of possibilities that may later be tested empirically.

In a similar vein Philip Manning (1989) identifies a tension between form and formlessness in Goffman's analyses. While Goffman's concepts provide a means of apprehending the world's stable features, there is a contrary impulse in Goffman that acknowledges that much escapes analysis and that sociological knowledge lacks secure foundations. Manning's notion of 'Goffman's spiral' suggests that Goffman's definitional labours are matched by efforts to explore the exceptions that undermine the classifications he produces. In a largely implicit way Goffman displays a sophisticated grasp of both the possibilities and the limits of his attempts to chart the interaction order.

The interpretations offered by Williams and Manning are consonant with Goffman's own conviction that a general theory of the interaction order was at the very least premature – in Goffman's (1961a: xiv) apt image, 'better ... different coats to clothe the children well than a single splendid tent in which they all shiver'. Once again, we come back to Goffman's preoccupation with systematics but disinterest in constructing a single, general theory of interaction.

TEXTUALITY

Goffman's writings are, quite simply, remarkable texts. His sociological methods cannot be treated in isolation from the textual devices which act as the medium of his analyses. At the centre of what Peter K. Manning (1976) terms Goffman's 'socio-literary method' is his imaginative and inventive use of metaphor and Kenneth Burke's (1965[1935]) method of 'perspective by incongruity'.

Apart from the major metaphors of drama, game and ritual, Goffman also uses figures such as the confidence trick, the Chinese conception of face and ethological analogies to effect his sociological analyses.

Goffman used these metaphors productively by mobilizing them in a manner that made evident both their potential and their limits (Williams 1998). Perspective by incongruity proposes that understanding is achieved by ironically juxtaposing terms and concepts that are not usually found together. A deliberate dissociation of ideas is sought through 'planned misnomers' that wrench loose the customary understandings associated with words. Sometimes Goffman deploys perspective by incongruity at the sub-sentence level (e.g. boys of eight to fourteen and other profane persons' (1959: 123); 'a New York specialist in the arts of vagrancy' 1963b: 44), sometimes in longer expressions (e.g. 'A person is a thing of which too much can be asked, and if everything must be asked, it will be at the asker's peril' (1969a: 42); 'Those who break the rules of interaction commit their crimes in jail' (1967: 115)). These literary devices are no mere stylistic embellishments. They are the direct means through which his conceptual advances are made. One consequence of the so-called crisis of representation is a heightened interest in textual dimensions of sociological analyses. Unsurprisingly, Goffman has attracted attention in these terms.

The earliest efforts to grapple with Goffman's textuality concentrated upon his use of theatrical, ritual and game metaphors. Versions of the thesis that metaphor is a means of sociological discovery recur in discussions of Goffman's metaphorical practice. Richard Brown claims that metaphor constitutes data in a 'symbolic realism' that affords 'no criteria for comparing metaphors with some absolute reality' (Brown 1977: 99). Yet sceptics seem to want analyses that are less fanciful, more literal. Rodney Watson (1999) for instance, sees Goffman's metaphorical usages as unavoidably parasitic on practical reasoning and as such amenable to ethnomethodological analysis. Goffman develops 'instructed readings' of interactional data that lead to ironicized sociological redescriptions. Watson uses membership categorization analysis to excavate the everyday logic readers necessarily employ in fitting Goffman's concepts to his examples to make those examples 'illustrations' of the concepts.

Those more sympathetic to the power of metaphor and other literary devices in sociological analysis have also endeavoured to disinter the layers of rhetoric at work in Goffman's texts. Paul Atkinson (1989) identifies similarities between Freud's style and Goffman's at the level of 'parataxis' (the sequencing and positioning of items or phrases within a text), which he thinks is the key to a more detailed reading of Goffman's textuality than irony, metaphor or Burkean perspective by incongruity. Through a close analysis of two extracts Atkinson shows how Goffman's imaginative ordering of listed items is a kind of bricolage, signifying a sociological world that, as in literary works, cannot be separated from the text. Goffman's artful use of rhetorical features allows him to cultivate the reader's sensibilities towards his topic-matter and thus to persuade as well as analyse.

Goffman has been seen as a sociological *farceur*, a writer attuned to life's comedic dimensions. Gary Alan Fine and Daniel Martin (1990) dissect the humorous tropes of sarcasm, satire, and irony deployed in *Asylums*. When applied to the analysis of the mentally ill, however, the fundamental ambiguity of these tropes places real and sometimes difficult demands on the reader who must work to recognize the seriousness of the critique embedded in his ethnographic writing.

In *Asylums* Goffman's vaunted 'partisan view' draws the attentive reader into his text. But throughout Goffman's work his remarkable capacity to co-opt the reader into seeing the world in his way is everywhere evident. Ricca Edmondson (1984) pays particular attention to this feature of Goffman's textual persuasiveness, showing how the development of his sociological analyses depends upon an engagement with his readers' opinions through the development of a distinct point of view. In this interpretation of Goffman's rhetoric, conceptual innovation in sociology is not simply an intellectual exercise: it is about changing readers' perceptions.

Some commentators argue that narrative voice is central to under-standing Goffman's methods. Comparing and contrasting Goffman's voice to that of Harold Garfinkel, Ira Cohen and Mary Rogers (1994) show how the playfulness and occasional vulnerability of Goffman's voice is likely to establish his credibility with readers. It is as if Goffman makes a direct plea to the reader's indulgence as that reader follows Goffman's 'sociological muse'. Philip Manning also identifies differing 'voices' to be heard in Goffman's writings. In much of his writing Goffman seems to be an 'essential copyist', committed to accurately reporting an objective social reality, yet there are moments when another voice breaks through, one that resists any such closure. Occasionally, a third voice emerges between the other two, 'remorselessly parodying every constructive suggestion' (Manning 1989: 228).

The persuasiveness of Goffman's voice also impresses Patricia Clough (1992). Her postmodern interpretation of Goffman's textuality detects affinities with deconstructionist themes. Working back from a footnote to Derrida in 'Felicity's condition' (Goffman 1983b), Clough links the idiosyncrasy of Goffman's ethnographic approach – an accumulation of concepts and their illustrations rather than the developing narrative of classical ethnography – to the 'commercial realism' that he identifies as the dominant discourse of contemporary advertising. Clough suggests that readers must submit to the flow of information provided in the illustration to appreciate the scope of the concept's applicability in the particular instance. The result is not the representation of reality but the production of a 'reality effect', a simulation of interaction comparable with a computer display. Working in a manner analogous to computer displays, Goffman's texts are judged to resist the narrative closure of realist ethnography. His writing takes us, in Clough's view, to the brink of the crisis of sociological description, but no further. For Clough, therefore, Goffman stands as 'the last great sociological ethnographer'.

While novel at the time he introduced them, Goffman's textual practices anticipate what has come to be known as the rhetorical turn in the social sciences (Clifford and Marcus 1986) and its associated critique of conventional social scientific notions of realism and objectivity. For Goffman commentators, issues of sociological method are very much bound up with the textual formats of his writing. Attention to the rhetorical dimension thus allows us to appreciate in detail how Goffman persuasively communicates his understandings of the social world to his readers.

9

After Goffman

The writings Goffman produced in the decade following his 1953 PhD dissertation possess a coherence and unity to be expected from a relatively youthful writer newly in command of an immensely successful analytical strategy trained on a novel topic matter. The project begins to waver in the mid- to late 1960s as the original seam is worked out and Goffman needed to find new resources to take forward his sociological venture. Around this time Goffman faced the challenge posed by Garfinkel's ethnomethodology and especially the conversation analysis of Sacks, Schegloff and Jefferson who showed that a terrain similar to Goffman's own could be investigated by rigorous empirical techniques. The use of transcribed taped data made the observation of interactional particulars more a matter of discipline than a talented eye and permitted the discovery of reproducible findings. Goffman's star began to rise again following his relocation to the East Coast and the publication of *Frame Analysis*. The sociolinguistic influences of Labov, Hymes and others around the University of Pennsylvania stimulated 'fresh talk' from Goffman. It is difficult to guess how Goffman's project might have developed had he lived longer. The casino research might have been written up in full, but he was already 15 years away from the fieldwork. There might have been a greater engagement with bodies of data such as the advertising images used in *Gender Advertisements* or the 'bloopers' extensively referred to in 'Radio talk'. But given the distinctiveness of the formal, conceptual approach that Goffman had developed to this point, any drastic shift in analytical strategy seems unlikely. Although there was much to clarify and consolidate from his earlier work, 'never look back' seems to have been the watchword of his mode of intellectual production.

Any overall assessment of Goffman's sociology quickly leads to legacy talk. What should be done with this impressive monument apart from admiring or dismissing it? The question continues to provoke because his ideas resist wholesale absorption by sociology's established theoretical and methodological approaches. The best general image to invoke remains the cash legacy notion of Georg Simmel, one of Goffman's acknowledged masters. When Simmel spoke towards the end of his life of his ideas as a cash legacy, to be spent as successors considered fit, it was to indicate that the product might no longer reveal its source. In what ways has Goffman provided resources for current sociological and other social scientific work? To properly address this question would require substantial documentation. In the brief space allotted here it is only possible to give a highly selective sketch of the scope of Goffman's influence.

Taking the headings used in this book, we can begin to get a rough estimate of his legacy. His work on the interaction order has helped sensitize generations of students to taken-for-granted aspects of interactional conduct. There have been a large number of dramaturgical studies of funerals, gynaecological examinations, political figures and behaviour, and the like (Brissett and Edgley 1990) that highlight the performed aspects of many work settings. Psychologists have made impression management into a distinct empirical orientation. Sociological research on public places would have hardly begun without Goffman's conceptualizations on unfocused and focused interaction (Cahill 1994). Goffman's ritual notions, especially his sophisticated understanding of face-work, has inspired many cross-cultural sociolinguistic studies of politeness behaviour, especially through Brown and Levinson's (1987[1978]) influential theory (Ting Toomey 1994). Alternative conceptualizations of politeness have also been indebted to Goffman (Bargiela-Chiappini 2003). Randall Collins (1980; 1988) has done much to excavate Goffman's Durkheimianism. Collins' (2004) general theory of interaction ritual chains directs attention to the emotionally energizing or enervating effects of successful and failed interaction rituals.

Frame analysis and the later concept of footing, often under the name of participant alignment, has become an important conceptual resource for interaction analysis. After a somewhat shaky start, frame analysis has made a substantial impact on social movement theory (Benford and Snow 2000), cognitive science and media studies, even though the link to Goffman's original formulation is becoming increasingly tenuous. (Goffman anticipated this situation in 1981, noting that Deborah Tannen had written a paper on frame that 'very little considers frame in my sense – or Bateson's' (1981b: 67).) The *Social Science Citation Index* shows that *Frame Analysis* is now highly referenced, scoring nearly twice as many citations as Durkheim's *Rules* over the past decade (Koenig 2004).

The impact of Goffman's studies of mental patients on deinstitution-alization policies has already been discussed. What has not been given the attention it deserves is Goffman's ambivalence about the 'community containment' alternative to the mental hospital. *Stigma* has also proved an enormously influential work. Perhaps the finest piece of formal sociology Goffman wrote, it has been especially influential among health researchers. It is also a pivotal text for groups advancing the interests of the differently abled. Goffman's work on gender has been unevenly taken up. *Gender Advertisements* became an instant classic of visual sociology and spawned dozens of studies seeking to test the patterning Goffman uncovered. Yet the theory of gender difference that underpinned the study has often been overlooked. Candace West (1996) has argued that in these writings and in his interaction sociology more generally, Goffman's great gift to feminist theory was to open the 'personal' to detailed sociological scrutiny.

At the beginning of the twenty-first century, after post-structuralism and deconstruction, Goffman's thinking about the individual is perhaps no longer so corrosive of commonsense understandings. His emphasis on the embodied characteristics of the interactant has led to his rediscovery by sociologists of the body. His brief essay on embarrassment made a major impact on the emergence of the sociology of emotion. Goffman's writings on the individual expand the scope of the notion of social being and represent a continuing challenge to comfortable conceptions of personal identity.

Despite the many idiosyncracies of Goffman's methods, here too he has made an impact. Long ago Robert Park emphasized the importance of first-hand observation for sociological inquiry. But it was Goffman who provided the training manual in sociological microscopy, helping the student of society to notice conduct that might otherwise escape attention. His ideas act as tools for perception, showing us how close observation is done. In a discipline dominated by large-scale quantitative studies he showed how pattern could be found in the details of people's ordinary conduct. His analyses provide readers with an accelerated understanding of the basic features of the interaction order. His distinctive development of Simmel's formal method also helped to loosen mid-twentieth century methodological orthodoxies. His highly personal style contributed to significant shifts in sociological understanding and practice. While his analyses remain rooted in realist assumptions, his sociological grasp of irony and perspective by incongruity sensitized sociologists to issues of representation embedded in their textual formats. His use of these tropes yields a distinctive kind of sociological criticism that gets its power from its understatement and the deadpan irony of his conceptual coinages.

At the heart of Goffman's contribution to social science is his conception of the interaction order. This 'layer' of social reality makes assertions of one-sided structural or agentic views of social life look impossibly simple-minded. Goffman (1983a) drew out a novel view of the micro-macro relation hinted at in earlier works. If Goffman's topic matter is 'the elementary forms of social life' (Jacobsen and Kristiansen 2002), what is its relation to what are sometimes seen as 'wider' or 'grander' social structures? First, Goffman never claims that larger social structures are built up from the interaction. Some social phenomena – Goffman mentions the ethnic succession in a municipal administration – are not simply reducible to what transpires interactionally. If social structures are not determined in any simple sense by interaction practices, then so too are interaction practices not straightforwardly determined by social structures. He suggested that the interaction order was surrounded by a metaphorical membrane that sifted and sorted the person's characteristics deriving from wider social orders (economic advantage, cultural capital, kin roles and the like) that would be permitted to be relevant in this encounter. There was, he suggested, no neat meshing of social structures and interactional cogs but rather a 'loosely-coupled' relationship between the interaction order and other social orders. This novel formulation of the micro-macro problem does not deny the importance of extra-situational matters. However, it does make their relevance an empirical question, something that has to be demonstrated in any particular instance. This is an interesting resolution of the micro-macro problem because it turns the common 'neglect of social structure' criticism into an empirical question that will not admit any generalized answer. This transforms a general question about the interaction order into particular questions about interaction orders. Although he never claimed the mantle of theorist, Goffman was always theoretically astute.

It is not surprising, therefore, that he has been described as a modernist standing in the vanguard of the postmodern, or that Goffman's ideas play an important role in the grand syntheses of Giddens and Habermas. The primarily conceptual character of Goffman's legacy has made it adaptable to a variety of analytic and empirical enterprises. But that has also been a major weakness, and conversation analytic critics are right to stress how Goffman's neglect of method left his project exposed. The absence of clear guidelines for conducting investigations of the interaction order perhaps explains why Goffman has many admirers but so few followers. Goffman's trademark – empirically attentive conceptual work – has proved just too tough for almost anyone but Goffman.

In this book I have tried to concentrate on Goffman's questions in order to highlight the logic of his analyses. This approach emphasizes Goffman the formal sociologist, the conceptual provider and articulator, at the expense of more diffuse understandings that arise from readers' direct acquaintance with his texts. While Goffman's writings were not always transparent, they remain immensely readable and highly quotable. Collins (1988) has argued that Goffman's writings are 'deep' in that they can be appreciated at many levels, according to the knowledge and attitudes of the reader. From this it follows, as Mary Rogers (2003) has suggested, that part of Goffman's legacy is to be misunderstood, and not just by his critics. Goffman was one of the few truly inspirational thinkers of modern sociology because, as Eliot Friedson (1983: 362) notes, his writings are suffused with a distinct 'moral sensibility' that 'shows us more of humanity than we could otherwise see'. Goffman's project instigated a permanent shift in the kind of perception that sociology could achieve. Sociology after Goffman is not quite the same as it was before.

Further Reading

There is no substitute for reading Goffman in the original. The delicacy of his insights are easily lost in summary. Most of Goffman's books are still in print and available in paperback. Of the books, *The Presentation of Self in Everyday Life* sets out Goffman's abiding sociological concerns and characteristic analytical approach. 'On face-work' (reprinted in *Interaction Ritual*) is an unsurpassed paper that offers a subtle statement of Goffman's ritual model. It has been particularly influential on politeness studies within pragmatics, providing a model for cross-cultural analysis of interpersonal conduct. Among Goffman's late work, 'Footing' (in *Forms of Talk*) and 'The interaction order' his valedictory 1982 American Sociological Association presidential address are not to be missed, along with his sole direct response to his critics, 'A reply to Denzin and Keller' (*Contemporary Sociology*, 1981). In a single volume, Charles Lemert and Ann Branaman's *The Goffman Reader* (Blackwell, 1997) offers an excellent collection of extracts from the full range of Goffman's books and papers. It also has two excellent introductory essays contextualizing Goffman's contribution.

Goffman's discouragement of critical interest in his ideas did not stop the development of a small industry devoted to the examination of his ideas. Jason Ditton's edited 1980 book, *The View from Goffman* (Macmillan) has cogent essays on the overall character and development of Goffman's thinking and contains much sound commentary, particularly in the chapters on frames, power, and talk.

Goffman's death in 1982 occasioned an explosion of critical interest extending well beyond customary obituary notices. Journals including *Theory and Society* (vol. 13 no.5, 1984) and *Theory, Culture and Society* (vol. 2 no.1, 1983) devoted special sections to reflective essays on his life and work. Memorial articles by Collins (1986), Friedson (1983), Hymes (1984), Lofland (1984) Marx (1984) and Strong (1983) shed important light on both the life and the work. A major Goffman conference held in York (UK) in 1986 led to two edited collections. Several contributions to the volume, *Erving Goffman: Exploring the Interaction Order*, edited by Paul Drew and Anthony Wootton (Polity, 1988) critically examine Goffman's aim to establish the sociology of the interaction order. York conference papers were also represented in a special issue on Goffman's sociology of *Human Studies* (vol. 12, nos 1–2, 1989) edited by Frances C. Waksler. Also around this time a conference in Mysore, India led to Stephen Riggins' multidisciplinary edited collection, *Beyond Goffman: Studies on Communication, Institution and Social Interaction* (Mouton de Gruyter, 1990).

Two monographs devoted to Goffman's ideas appeared in 1992. Philip Manning's *Erving Goffman and Modern Sociology* (Polity) offered a well-crafted and accessible outline of Goffman's principal ideas. Tom Burns, whose personal acquaintance with Goffman went back to his Edinburgh days, published *Erving Goffman* (Routledge), a commentary whose detail and substance have yet to be surpassed. In this 386-page volume, Burns combines shrewd insights into Goffman's work with impressive attention to its detail.

Gary Alan Fine and Greg Smith's four volume *Erving Goffman*, published in 2000 in the Sage Masters of Modern Social Thought, contains over 90 key contributions to the critical literature through to the end of the twentieth century. Fresh views of Goffman's legacy can be found in the papers collected in Greg Smith's *Goffman and Social Organization* (Routledge 1999) and A. Javier Treviño's *Goffman's Legacy* (Rowman & Littlefield 2003). A former student of Goffman's, Thomas Scheff, presents a singular interpretation of his work in *Goffman Unbound! A New Paradigm for Social Science* (Boulder, CO: Paradigm Publishers, 2006). Scheff argues that Goffman's vision centres on his discovery of the emotional/relational world made vivid in social situations.

Goffman ensured there would be no archive for scholars to ponder. Its absence closes many doors for the biographer. However, Yves Winkin has undertaken substantial biographical work, including a large number of interviews with Goffman's friends, colleagues and students. Winkin's (1988) intellectual biography of Goffman in French tracks his life and work down to 1959. A full biography in English is awaited; elements have been presented as Winkin (1999) and Winkin (2000). Goffman was a reluctant interviewee. The interview he granted another Belgian social scientist, Jef Verhoeven, in 1980 (Verhoeven 1993) contains many intriguing asides and insights into how Goffman saw his sociological project and neighbouring sociologies.

References

Anderson, R.J., Hughes, J.A. and Sharrock, W.W. (1985) *The Sociology Game: An Introduction to Sociological Reasoning*, London: Longman.

Atkinson, P. (1989) 'Goffman's poetics', *Human Studies* 12: 59–76.

Austin, J.L. (1962) *How to Do Things With Words*, Oxford: Clarendon.

Bargiela-Chiappini, F. (2003) 'Face and politeness: (new) insights for (old) concepts', *Journal of Pragmatics* 35: 1453–69.

Barnard, C. (1947) *The Functions of the Executive*, Cambridge, MA: Harvard University Press.

Battershill, C. (1990) 'Erving Goffman as a precursor to post-modern sociology', in S.H. Riggins (ed.) *Beyond Goffman: Studies on Communication, Institution, and Social Interaction*, Berlin: Mouton de Gruyter.

Becker, H.S. (1953) 'Becoming a marihuana user', *American Journal of Sociology* 59: 235–42.

—— (2003) 'The politics of presentation: Goffman and total institutions', *Symbolic Interaction* 26: 659–69.

Benford, R.D. and Snow, D.A. (2000) 'Framing processes and social movements: an overview and assessment', *Annual Review of Sociology* 26: 611–39.

Berger, B. (1986) 'Foreword', in E. Goffman, *Frame Analysis: An Essay on the Organization of Experience*, Boston, MA: Northeastern University Press.

Birdwhistell, R.L. (1971) *Kinesics and Context: Essays on Body-Motion Communication*, London: Allen Lane.

Blumer. H. (1969) *Symbolic Interactionism: Perspective and Method*, Englewood Cliffs, NJ: Prentice-Hall.

Brissett, D. and Edgley, C. (eds) (1990) *Life as Theater: A Dramaturgical Sourcebook*, 2nd edn, New York: Aldine de Gruyter.

Brown, R.H. (1977) *A Poetic for Sociology: Toward a Logic of Discovery for the Human Sciences*, Cambridge: Cambridge University Press.

Brown, S. C. and Levinson, P. (1987) *Politeness: Some Universals of Language Use*, Cambridge: Cambridge University Press.

Burke, K. (1965[1935]) *Permanence and Change*, Indianapolis: Bobbs-Merrill.

Burns, T. (1992) *Erving Goffman*, London: Routledge.

Butler, J. (1990) *Gender Trouble*, London: Routledge.

Cahill, S.E. (1994) 'Following Goffman, following Durkheim into the public realm', *Research in Community Sociology*, Supplement 1: 3–17.

—— (1998) 'Toward a sociology of the person' *Sociological Theory* 16: 131–48.

Caudill, W. (1962) Review of *Asylums*, *American Journal of Sociology* 68: 366–9.

Charmaz, K. (2004) 'Premises, principles, and practices in qualitative research: revisiting the foundations', *Qualitative Health Research* 14: 976–93.

Chriss, J.J. (1999) 'Role distance and the negational self', in G. Smith (ed.) *Goffman and Social Organization: Studies in a Sociological Legacy*, London: Routledge.

Cioffi, F. (2000) 'The propaedeutic delusion: what can "ethogenic science" add to our pre-theoretic understanding of "loss of dignity, humiliation and expressive failure"?', *History of the Human Sciences* 13: 108–23.

Clayman, S.E. (1992) 'Footing in the achievement of neutrality: the case of news-interview discourse', in P. Drew and J. Heritage (eds) *Talk at Work: Interaction in Institutional Settings*, Cambridge: Cambridge University Press.

Clifford, J. and Marcus G.E. (eds) (1986) *Writing Culture: The Poetics and Politics of Ethnography*, Berkeley: University of California Press.

Clough, P.T. (1992) *The End(s) of Ethnography*, Newbury Park, CA: Sage.

Cohen, I.J. and Rogers, M.F. (1994) 'Autonomy and credibility: voice as method', *Sociological Theory* 12, 3: 304–18.

Collins, R. (1980) 'Erving Goffman and the development of modern social theory', in J. Ditton (ed.) *The View from Goffman,* London and Basingstoke: Macmillan.

—— (1986) 'The passing of intellectual generations: reflections on the death of Erving Goffman', *Sociological Theory* 4: 106–113.

—— (1988) 'Theoretical continuities in Goffman's work', in P. Drew and A. Wootton (eds) *Erving Goffman: Exploring the Interaction Order*, Cambridge: Polity.

—— (2004) *Interaction Ritual Chains*, Princeton, NJ: Princeton University Press.

Cooley, C. H. (1909) *Social Organization: A Study of the Larger Mind*, New York: Scribner's.

Coser, L.A. (1956) *The Functions of Social Conflict*, London: Routledge and Kegan Paul.

Crossley, N. (1995) 'Body techniques, agency and intercorporeality: on Goffman's *Relations in Public*', *Sociology* 29: 133–49.

Cuzzort, R.P. (1969) *Humanity and Sociological Theory*, New York: Holt, Rinehart and Winston.

Czyzewski, M. (1987) 'Erving Goffman on the individual: a reconstruction', *Polish Sociological Bulletin* 79: 31–41.

Dahrendorf, R. (1973) *Homo Sociologicus*, London: Routledge and Kegan Paul.

David, P. (1980) 'The reluctant self-presentation of Erving Goffman', *Times Higher Education Supplement* 19 September: 7.

Davies, C. (1989) 'Goffman's concept of the total institution', *Human Studies* 12: 77–96.

Denzin, N.K and Keller, C.M. (1981) '*Frame Analysis* reconsidered', *Contemporary Sociology* 10: 52–60.

Durkheim, E. (1915) *The Elementary Forms of the Religious Life*, London: Allen & Unwin.

—— (1969) 'Individualism and the intellectuals', *Political Studies* 17: 14–30.

Edgley, C. (2003) 'The dramaturgical genre', in L.T. Reynolds an N.J. Herman-Kinney (eds) *Handbook of Symbolic Interactionism*, Walnut Creek, CA: Altamira.

Edmondson, R. (1984) *Rhetoric in Sociology*, London: Macmillan.

Fairbrother, P. (1977) 'Experience and trust in sociological work', *Sociology* 11:359–68.

Fine, G.A. and Martin, D. (1990) 'A partisan view: sarcasm, satire and irony as voices in Erving Goffman's *Asylums*', *Journal of Contemporary Ethnography* 19: 89–115.

Frank, A.W. (1979) 'Reality construction in sociology', *Annual Review of Sociology* 5: 167–91.

Friedson, E. (1983) 'Celebrating Erving Goffman', *Contemporary Sociology* 12: 359–62.

Gamson, W.A. (1975) Review of *Frame Analysis, Contemporary Sociology* 4: 603–7.

Gardner, C.B. (1989) 'Analyzing gender in public places: rethinking Goffman's vision of everyday life', *The American Sociologist* 20: 42–56.

—— (1995) *Passing By: Gender and Public Harassment*, Berkeley, CA: University of California Press.

Geertz, Clifford (1980) 'Blurred genres: the refiguration of social thought', *The American Scholar* 29: 165–79.

Glaser, B.G. and Strauss, A.L. (1967) *The Discovery of Grounded Theory*, Chicago: Aldine.

Goffman, E. (1949) Some characteristics of response to depicted experience, MA thesis, Department of Sociology, University of Chicago.

—— (1951) 'Symbols of class status', *British Journal of Sociology* 2: 294–304.

—— (1952) 'On cooling the mark out: some aspects of adaptation to failure', *Psychiatry* 15: 451–63.

—— (1953a) Communication conduct in an island community, PhD dissertation, Department of Sociology, University of Chicago.

—— (1953b) 'The service station dealer: the man and his work', Mimeographed report prepared for the American Petroleum Institute. Chicago, IL: Social Research Incorporated.

—— (1955) 'On face-work: an analysis of ritual elements in social interaction', *Psychiatry* 18: 213–31. Reprinted in Goffman (1967).

—— (1956a) *The Presentation of Self in Everyday Life*, Edinburgh: University of Edinburgh, Social Sciences Research Centre.

—— (1956b) 'Embarrassment and social organization', *American Journal of Sociology* 62: 264–71. Reprinted in Goffman (1967).

—— (1956c) 'The nature of deference and demeanor', *American Anthropologist* 58: 473–502. Reprinted in Goffman (1967).

—— (1957a) 'Alienation from interaction', *Human Relations* 10: 47–59. Reprinted in Goffman (1967).

—— (1957b) 'On some convergences of sociology and psychiatry', *Psychiatry* 20: 201–3.

—— (1957c) 'Some dimensions of the problem', in M. Greenblatt, D.J. Levinson and R.H. Williams (eds) *The Patient and the Mental Hospital*, New York: The Free Press of Glencoe.

—— (1957d) Book review of D.R. Cressey, *Other People's Money, Psychiatry* 20: 321–6.

—— (1959) *The Presentation of Self in Everyday Life*, New York: Doubleday, Anchor Books.

—— (1961a) *Asylums: Essays on the Social Situation of Mental Patients and Other Inmates*, New York: Doubleday, Anchor Books.

—— (1961b) *Encounters: Two Studies in the Sociology of Interaction*, Indianapolis: Bobbs-Merrill.

—— (1963a) *Behavior in Public Places: Notes on the Social Organization of Gatherings*, New York: The Free Press.

—— (1963b) *Stigma: Notes on the Management of Spoiled Identity*, Englewood Cliffs NJ: Prentice-Hall.

—— (1964) Discussion of 'Mental symptoms and public order', *Disorders of Communication*, Association for Research in Nervous and Mental Disease, Research Publications, 42: 283–9.

—— (1967) *Interaction Ritual: Essays on Face-to-Face Behavior*, New York: Doubleday, Anchor Books.

—— (1969a) *Strategic Interaction*, Philadelphia, PA: University of Pennsylvania Press.

—— (1969b) 'The insanity of place', *Psychiatry* 32: 357–88. Reprinted in Goffman (1971).

—— (1971) *Relations in Public: Microstudies of the Public Order*, New York: Basic Books.

—— (1974) *Frame Analysis: An Essay on the Organization of Experience*, Cambridge MA: Harvard University Press.

—— (1977) 'The arrangement between the sexes', *Theory and Society* 4: 301–32.

—— (1979) *Gender Advertisements*, London: Macmillan.

—— (1981a) *Forms of Talk*, Oxford: Basil Blackwell.

—— (1981b) 'A reply to Denzin and Keller', *Contemporary Sociology* 10: 60–8.

—— (1981c) 'Program committee encourages papers on range of methodologies', *ASA Footnotes* 9:4.

—— (1983a) 'The interaction order', *American Sociological Review* 48: 1–17.

—— (1983b) 'Felicity's condition', *American Journal of Sociology* 89: 1–53.

—— (1989) 'On fieldwork', transcribed by L.H. Lofland, *Journal of Contemporary Ethnography* 18: 123–32.

Gonos, G. (1977) '"Situation" vs. "frame": The "interactionist" and the "structuralist" analyses of everyday life', *American Sociological Review* 42: 854–67.

—— (1980) 'The class position of Goffman's sociology: social origins of an American structuralism', in J. Ditton (ed.) *The View From Goffman*, London: Macmillan.

Gouldner, A. (1970) *The Coming Crisis of Western Sociology*, New York: Basic Books.

Greenblatt, M., Levinson, D.J. and Williams, R.H. (1957) *The Patient and the Mental Hospital: Contributions of Research in the Science of Social Behavior*, Glencoe, IL: The Free Press.

Gronfein, W. (1992) 'Goffman's *Asylums* and the social control of the mentally ill', *Perspectives on Social Problems* 4: 129–53.

—— (1999) 'Sundered selves: mental illness and the interaction order in the work of Erving Goffman', in G. Smith (ed.) *Goffman and Social Organization: Studies in a Sociological Legacy*, London and New York: Routledge.

Hazelrigg, L. (1992) 'Reading Goffman's framing as provocation of a discipline', *Human Studies* 15: 239–64.

Helmer, J. (1970) 'The face of the man without qualities', *Social Research* 37: 547–79.

Hochschild, A.R. (1983) *The Managed Heart: Commercialization of Human Feeling*, Berkeley, CA: University of California Press.

Hoffman, J. (1957) 'Problems of administration in a large mental hospital', in M. Greenblatt, D.J. Levinson and R.H. Williams (eds) *The Patient and the Mental Hospital*, New York: The Free Press of Glencoe.

Hughes, E.C. (1945) 'Dilemmas and contradictions of status', *American Journal of Sociology* 50: 353–9.

Hymes, D. (1984) 'On Erving Goffman', *Theory and Society* 13: 621–31.

Ichheiser, G. (1949) 'Misunderstandings in human relations: a study of false social perception', supplement to *American Journal of Sociology*, 55(2).

Jacobsen, M.H. and Kristiansen, S. (2002) *Erving Goffman: Sociologien om det Elementaere Livs Sociale Former*, Copenhagen: Hans Reitzels Forlag.

Jameson, F. (1976) 'On Goffman's frame analysis', *Theory and Society* 3(1): 119–33.

Jaworski, G.D. (2000) 'Erving Goffman: the reluctant apprentice', *Symbolic Interaction* 23: 299–308.

Koenig, T. (2004) 'Frame analysis: a primer', available at: http://www.lboro. ac.uk/research/mmethods/resources/links/frames_primer.html

Lemert, E.M. (1972) *Human Deviance, Social Problems and Social Control*, Englewood Cliffs, NJ: Prentice Hall.

Levinson, S.C. (1988) 'Putting linguistics on a proper footing: explorations in Goffman's concepts of participation', in P. Drew and A. Wootton (eds) *Erving Goffman: Exploring the Interaction Order*, Cambridge: Polity.

Levy, S. (2003) 'Roots of marketing and consumer research at the University of Chicago', *Consumption, Markets and Culture* 6: 99–110.

Lofland, J. (1984) 'Erving Goffman's sociological legacies', *Urban Life* 13: 7–34.

Lofland, L.H. (1998) *The Public Realm: Exploring the City's Quintessential Public Territory*, New York: Aldine de Gruyter.

Lyman, S.M. and Scott, M.B. (1970) *A Sociology of the Absurd*, New York: Appleton-Century-Crofts.

MacIntyre, A. (1981) *After Virtue: A Study in Moral Theory*, London: Duckworth.

Manning, P.K. (1976) 'The decline of civility: a comment on Erving Goffman's sociology', *Canadian Review of Sociology and Anthropology* 13: 13–25.

Manning, P. (1989) 'Resemblances', *History of the Human Sciences* 2: 207–33.

—— (1992) *Erving Goffman and Modern Sociology*, Cambridge: Polity Press.

—— (1999) 'The institutionalization and deinstitutionalization of the mentally ill: lessons from Goffman', in J.J. Chriss (ed.) *Counseling and the Therapeutic State*, Chicago, IL: Aldine.

Marx, G.T. (1984) 'Role models and role distance: a remembrance of Erving Goffman', *Theory and Society* 13: 649–62.

Mead, G.H. (1934) *Mind, Self and Society, From the Standpoint of A Social Behaviorist*, Chicago, IL: University of Chicago Press.

Mechanic, D. (1989) 'Medical sociology: some tensions among theory, method and substance', *Journal of Health and Social Behaviour* 30: 147–60.

Meltzer, B.N., Petras, J.W. and Reynolds, L.T. (1975) *Symbolic Interactionism: Genesis, Varieties and Criticism*, London: Routledge and Kegan Paul.

Messinger, S.L. with Sampson, H. and Towne, R.D. (1962) 'Life as theater: some notes on the dramaturgic approach to social reality', *Sociometry* 25: 98–110.

Miller, T.G. (1984) 'Goffman, social acting and moral behavior', *Journal for the Theory of Social Behaviour* 14: 141–63.

—— (1986) 'Goffman, positivism and the self', *Philosophy of the Social Sciences* 16: 177–95.

Mouzelis, N. (1971) 'On total institutions', *Sociology* 5: 113–20.

Nussbaum, M.C. (2004) *Hiding from Humanity: Disgust, Shame and the Law*, Princeton: NJ: Princeton University Press.

Ostrow, J. (1996) 'Spontaneous involvement and social life', *Sociological Perspectives* 39: 341–51.

Owen, M. (1983) *Apologies and Remedial Interchanges*, Berlin: Mouton.

Parsons, T. (1951) *The Social System*, Glencoe, IL: Free Press.

Peele, R., Luisada, P.V., Lucas, M.J., Rudisell, D. and Taylor, D. (1977) '*Asylums* Revisited', *American Journal of Psychiatry* 134: 1077–81.

Perry, N. (1974) 'The two cultures and the total institution', *British Journal of Sociology* 25: 345–55.

Phillips, J. (1983) 'Goffman's linguistic turn: a comment on *Forms of Talk*', *Theory, Culture and Society* 2: 114–16.

Priest, M. (1998) personal communication, 18 October.

Psathas, G. and Waksler, F.C. (1973) 'Essential features of face-to-face interaction', in George Psathas (ed.) *Phenomenological Sociology: Issues and Applications*, New York: Wiley, pp. 159–83.

Rawls, A.W. (1987) 'The interaction order *sui generis*: Goffman's contribution to social theory', *Sociological Theory* 5: 136–49.

Rock, P. (1979) *The Making of Symbolic Interactionism*, London: Macmillan.

Rogers, M. (2003) 'The personal is dramaturgical (and political)', in J. Treviño (ed.) *Goffman's Legacy,* New York: Rowman and Littlefield.

Rowland, H. (1939) 'Segregated communities and mental health', in F.R. Moulton (ed.) *Mental Health Publications of the American Association for the Advancement of Science*, New York: American Association for the Advancement of Science.

Scheff, T.J. (2005) 'The structure of context: deciphering *Frame Analysis*', *Sociological Theory* 23: 368–85.

Schegloff, E.A. (1988) 'Goffman and the analysis of conversation', in P. Drew and A. Wootton (eds) *Erving Goffman: Exploring the Interaction Order*, Cambridge: Polity.

Schudson, M. (1984) 'Embarrassment and Erving Goffman's idea of human nature', *Theory and Society* 13: 633–48.

Schutz, A. (1962[1945]) 'On multiple realities', in *Collected Papers I.* (ed.) M. Natanson, The Hague: Martinus Nijhoff.

Schwalbe, M. L. (1993) 'Goffman against postmodernism: emotion and the reality of the self', *Symbolic Interaction* 16: 333–350.

Scull, A. (1989) *Social Order/Mental Disorder: Anglo-American Psychiatry in Historical Perspective*, Berkeley, CA: University of California Press.

Sedgwick, P. (1982) *Psychopolitics*, London: Pluto.

Sennett, R. (1977) *The Fall of Public Man*, Cambridge: Cambridge University Press.

Sharrock, W.W. (1976) 'Review of *Frame Analysis*', *Sociology* 10: 332–4.

Shilling, C. (1993) *The Body and Social Theory*, London: Sage.

Siegler, M. and Osmond, H. (1971), 'Goffman's model of mental illness', *British Journal of Psychiatry* 119: 419–24.

Simmel, G. (1950) *The Sociology of Georg Simmel*, edited by K.H. Wolff, New York: The Free Press.

Smith, G.W.H. (1994[1989]) 'Snapshots sub specie aeternitatis: Simmel, Goffman and formal sociology', in D. Frisby (ed.) *Georg Simmel: Critical Assessments, Volume III*, London: Routledge.

—— (2003) 'Chrysalid Goffman: a note on "Some characteristics of response to depicted experience"', *Symbolic Interaction* 26: 645–58.

Spillius, E. Bott (1993) Personal communication. 9 December.

Strong, P.M. (1979) *The Ceremonial Order of the Clinic: Parents, Doctors and Medical Bureaucracies*, London: Routledge & Kegan Paul.

—— (1983) 'On the importance of being Erving: Erving Goffman, 1922–1982', *Sociology of Health and Illness* 5: 345–55.

Ting-Toomey, S. (ed.) (1994) *The Challenge of Facework: Cross-Cultural and Interpersonal Issues*, Albany, NY: State University of New York Press.

Travers, A. (1992) 'Strangers to themselves: how interactants are other than they are', *British Journal of Sociology* 43: 601–37.

Tseëlon, E. (1992) 'Is the presented self sincere? Goffman, impression management, and the postmodern self', *Theory, Culture & Society* 9, 2: 115–28.

Turner, B. S. (1984) *The Body and Society*, Oxford: Blackwell.

Verhoeven, J. (1993) 'An interview with Erving Goffman, 1980', *Research on Language and Social Interaction* 26: 317–48.

Warner, M.H. (1988) *W. Lloyd Warner: Social Anthropologist*, New York: Publishing Center for Cultural Resources.

Warner, W.L. and Henry, W.E. (1948) 'The radio daytime serial: a symbolic analysis', *Genetic Psychology Monographs* 37: 3–71.

Watson, R. (1999) 'Reading Goffman on interaction', in G. Smith (ed.) *Goffman and Social Organization*, London: Routledge.

Wedel, J.M. (1978) 'Ladies, we've been framed! Observations on Erving Goffman's "The arrangement between the sexes"', *Theory and Society* 5: 113–25.

Weigert, A. (1975) 'Substantival self: a primitive term for social psychology', *Philosophy of the Social Sciences* 5: 43–62.

Weinstein, R. M. (1994), 'Goffman's *Asylums* and the total institution model of mental hospitals', *Psychiatry* 57: 348–67.

West, C. (1996) 'Goffman in feminist perspective', *Sociological Perspectives* 39: 353–69.

West, C. and Zimmerman, D.H. (1977) 'Women's place in everyday talk: reflections on parent-child interaction', *Social Problems* 24: 521–9.

Williams, R. (1980) 'Goffman's sociology of talk', in J. Ditton (ed.) *The View From Goffman*, London and Basingstoke: Macmillan.

—— (1988) 'Understanding Goffman's methods', in P. Drew and A.Wootton (eds) *Erving Goffman: Exploring the Interaction Order*, Cambridge: Polity.

—— (1998) 'Erving Goffman', in R. Stones (ed.) *Key Sociological Thinkers*, Basingstoke and London: Macmillan.

Williamson, J. (1978) *Decoding Advertisements*, London: Marion Boyars.

Wilshire, B. (1982) *Role Playing and Identity: The Limits of Theatre as Metaphor*, Bloomington, IN: Indiana University Press.

Winkin, Y. (1984) 'Éléments pour une histoire sociale des sciences sociales Américaines: une chronique: entretien avec Erving Goffman', *Actes de la Recherche en Sciences Sociales* 54: 85–7.

—— (ed.) (1988) *Erving Goffman: Les Moments et Leurs Hommes,* Paris: Seuil/Minuit.

—— (1999) 'Erving Goffman: what is a life? The uneasy making of an intellectual biography', in G. Smith (ed.) *Goffman and Social Organization: Studies in a Sociological Legacy*, London: Routledge.

—— (2000[1992]) 'Baltasound as the symbolic capital of social interaction', in G.A. Fine and G.W.H. Smith (eds) *Erving Goffman* vol. 1, London: Sage.

Wrong, D. (1990) 'Imagining the real' in B.M. Berger (ed.) *Authors of Their Own Lives: Intellectual Autobiographies by Twenty American Sociologists*, Berkeley, CA and Los Angeles, CA: University of California Press.

Young, T.R. (1971) 'The politics of sociology: Gouldner, Goffman and Garfinkel', *The American Sociologist* 6: 276–81.

Zimmerman, D. (1989) 'Prendre position', in I. Joseph (ed.) *Le Parler Frais d'Erving Goffman*, Paris: Éditions de Minuit.

Index